PUFFIN BOOKS
GANDHI IN 150 ANECDOTES

ARTHY MUTHANNA SINGH is a children's writer, freelance journalist, copywriter, editor and cartoonist. She has authored more than thirty-five books for children. Currently, she is a partner at SYLLABLES27, an outfit that produces books for children on a turnkey basis for publishers and organizations that work with children.

MAMTA NAINY is a children's writer, editor and translator based in New Delhi, whose book *A Brush with Indian Art* won The Hindu Young World-Goodbooks Award 2019 for Best Book (Non-Fiction).

PUFFIN BOOKS

USA | Canada | UK | Ireland | Australia
New Zealand | India | South Africa | China

Puffin Books is part of the Penguin Random House group of companies
whose addresses can be found at global.penguinrandomhouse.com

Published by Penguin Random House India Pvt. Ltd
7th Floor, Infinity Tower C, DLF Cyber City,
Gurgaon 122 002, Haryana, India

First published in Puffin Books by Penguin Random House India 2019

Text copyright © Arthy Muthanna Singh and Mamta Nainy 2019
Illustrations copyright © Aniruddha Mukherjee and Charulata Mukherjee 2019

ISBN 9780143449225

Layout and Design by Aniruddha Mukherjee
Typeset in Droid Serif by Syllables27, New Delhi
Printed at Replika Press Pvt. Ltd.

www.penguin.co.in

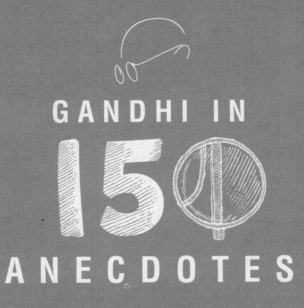

GANDHI IN
150
ANECDOTES

ARTHY MUTHANNA SINGH AND MAMTA NAINY

ILLUSTRATIONS BY ANIRUDDHA MUKHERJEE AND CHARULATA MUKHERJEE

PUFFIN BOOKS

An imprint of Penguin Random House

INTRODUCTION

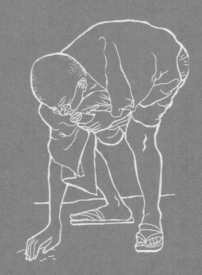

A Superhero with a Walking Stick

What makes a superhero? A superpower to save the world? A cool costume? A fancy name? Well, not really. What truly makes a superhero out of an ordinary person is the kindness in one's heart, the courage to stand up for oneself and those around us, the determination and perseverance to spark change and pave the way for a better world.

This Gandhi Jayanti, 2 October 2019, is special, for we're celebrating the 150th birth anniversary of one such superhero—Mohandas Karamchand Gandhi. A warrior of truth, a crusader of non-violence and the Father of Our Nation, this colossus of our freedom struggle was a true model of simplicity. With the barest of means, he took an empire head on and gave all of us our most prized possession—political freedom and social equality. But how could a small, frail man with just a walking stick and an unstinted faith in the idea of non-violence lead a country as huge as ours to independence? By living a remarkable life and following ideas that stemmed from a strong moral character, compassionate zeal and tremendous love for everyone, irrespective of their caste, creed, race or religion. These very traits provided him with the necessary fuel to keep the engine of his quiet, peaceful but immensely strong revolution going at an unfaltering pace. Through his calm, steady heroism, he changed everything for India and even inspired movements all over the world, proving that the smallest of us can be the most powerful!

This book highlights little-known—unusual, even—episodes from Gandhiji's life, giving everyone an insight into his mind and how it worked even in the most ordinary situations. His life goes on to show that what we make of the challenges we face is what decides what we will become. And this is not just a story of him; it's what we're all capable of on our best days. He could have been you or us.

You can open any page in this book and go back to an exciting time in our country's history, when one man made a life-changing difference to millions of lives. In fact, if you think about it, his life and ideologies have made a difference to each one of us—the very reason why he is so relevant even today and needs to be celebrated.

'My life is my message'

—Mahatma Gandhi

1 In the Family

Gandhiji was born on 2 October 1869 in Porbandar, Gujarat. Gandhiji's father, Karamchand, was a diwan, or minister, in the princely states of Porbandar and Rajkot. He was quite liberal and had friends from all religions. Gandhiji's mother, Putlibai, was a deeply pious woman who regularly visited temples and observed rigorous fasting. She lovingly called Gandhiji 'Mohania'. Gandhiji loved to tease his mother—he scribbled all over the floor with a chalk, long before he even learnt to write. Once, as a small child, he removed the idol of a god from the family prayer room so that he could sit there himself!

Afraid of the Dark

As a child, Gandhiji was afraid of the dark. He imagined that serpents, ghosts and thieves would emerge from the darkness of the room. One dark night, Gandhiji had to go from one room to another. As he stepped out of the room, his knees shook and his heart began to beat faster. A family maidservant was standing by the door.

'What's the matter, child?' she asked.

'I am frightened, Masi,' young Mohania answered.

'Of what?' she asked.

'Of darkness,' Mohania whispered. 'I'm afraid of serpents and ghosts!'

The maidservant patted the child's head affectionately and said, 'Think of Lord Rama and no snake or ghost will dare come near you.'

The maidservant's words gave Gandhiji courage. Chanting the name of Lord Rama, he left the room. And from that day on, he was never lonely or afraid.

3

Owning Up

When Gandhiji was young, his parents lovingly called him Mohania. He often got into mischief. Once, he and his friends tried to steal a statue from a temple but were caught by the temple priest. All his friends denied having any part in stealing the statue, but little Mohania owned up to it—a sure sign of becoming a 'Mahatma' or 'a great soul'.

A Compassionate Child

Gandhiji, from early childhood, always showed compassion for the injured and their suffering. His elder sister, Raliatbehn, recalled how young Mohania once climbed a guava tree in a neighbour's backyard, with strips of torn cloth, trying to bandage the broken skin on the fruits pecked at by birds.

5

Classroom and beyond

As a child, Gandhiji never liked going to school; it was a painful experience for him. He was not an outstanding student, was small for his age and extremely skinny. He had ears that stuck out awkwardly from his head. He lived in constant fear of being teased for his looks by his classmates. So, Gandhiji ran to school just in time for class to begin, and as soon as the lessons got over, he fled back home so that no one would see him.

In the Company of Books

Right from his childhood, Gandhiji loved reading and spent most of his time in the company of books. He once read a play in school. It was about a man named Shravan Kumar. Shravan was so devoted to his blind parents that when they were too old to travel, he made a weighing balance by seating them on two big baskets tied to the ends of a pole and carried them on a sling on his shoulder to take them on a pilgrimage to various holy places. It was an example that Gandhiji wanted to follow—one person carrying others who needed help. Another mythological tale that left a huge impact on Gandhiji was King Harishchandra's story. He was so moved by the king sacrificing his kingdom and his family to follow the path of truth that Gandhiji resolved to always be truthful.

7

Introduction to Untouchability

Gandhiji's family moved from Porbandar to Rajkot when he was seven years old. He found it extremely difficult to make new friends, as he was very shy. As soon as school was over, he would run home. At home, he became friends with Uka, a young boy who would come to their house to clean the toilets. His mother, Putlibai, was not happy with this. She objected to this friendship and insisted that he take a bath to 'cleanse' himself. Uka was an untouchable, she said. Even at that young age, Gandhiji knew she was wrong, but . . .

Truth or Truth?

When Gandhiji was in high school, one day, an educational inspector came to his class. He had set five words for the students to write in a spelling exercise. The third word was 'kettle'. Gandhiji misspelt the word as 'ketle'. While the inspector moved from student to student, the teacher saw that Gandhiji had spelt the word wrong. He touched Gandhiji's leg with his foot to get his attention. He even motioned with his eyes, hinting Gandhiji to look at his neighbour's slate, but Gandhiji didn't want to copy from anyone. The result was that all the boys, except Gandhiji, were found to have spelt every word correctly. When the inspector left the class, the teacher called Gandhiji and said, 'I told you to copy from your neighbour, but you wouldn't listen to me. You're a disgrace to my class!' Gandhiji said, 'I may be a disgrace, but I can't tell a lie.'

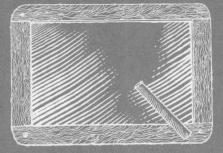

Experiments with Eating Meat

Gandhiji belonged to a devout Hindu family who never ate meat. When Gandhiji was young, he yielded to the temptation of eating meat for some time. He was urged by a friend to eat meat to gain the strength to 'defeat the British'. According to Gandhiji's friend, the Englishmen's power to dominate India was because of their superior strength that came from eating meat. So, Gandhiji started eating meat with his friend and enjoyed meat dishes. But then, a moral revulsion that he was cheating his parents came over him and he resolved never to eat meat again.

A Piece of Gold

When Gandhiji was a teenager, he once took to smoking—even going so far as to steal change from the servants to buy cigarettes and thereby incur debt! So, to pay off his increasing debt, he stole a piece of gold from the bracelet that his brother wore. But soon after, the wrongdoing weighed heavily on his conscience. Gandhiji wrote a confession letter to his father and asked him for the greatest possible punishment. He thought that his father would be livid with him, but instead he was moved to tears. Without uttering a word, Gandhiji's father tore the letter with a deep sigh. Gandhiji was deeply grieved. Tears rolled down his cheeks too, and he resolved to never steal again.

11

The Story of the Sacred Thread

Brahmins, the highest caste in the hierarchy of Hindu society, wear *janeu* or a sacred thread. Gandhiji belonged to the lower bania caste and as a young person, he always envied the Brahmins sporting their sacred threads, for he wanted to be one of them. But as he grew up, he realized the injustices of the caste system and went on to reform it in his bid for a more egalitarian society.

Gandhiji's Own Child Marriage

While Gandhiji objected to child marriages all his adult life, he himself was married at the age of thirteen. His brother Karsandas also got married on the same day. Gandhiji's bride was Kasturba Makhanji, a young girl with a mind of her own! 'Ba', as she was affectionately called by Gandhiji, did as she pleased.

13

Gandhiji's Father's Accident

On the way to Gandhiji's and Karsandas' weddings, their father, Karamchand Gandhi, met with an accident. The carriage he was travelling in toppled over and he was badly bruised. He arrived at the venue bandaged all over. While everyone else panicked, he would not hear of the weddings being postponed. The ceremonies and celebrations continued as planned. However, Karamchand Gandhi never fully recovered from those injuries and he had to spend a lot of time in bed because of that. Gandhiji would nurse his father every day in the evenings after he had completed his studies. This made him get closer to his father than ever before.

Double Tragedy

At the age of fifteen, Gandhiji was busy with his studies, being a husband to a wife expecting a baby and looking after his father. He had hardly any time to spare. Soon tragedy struck. One night, his beloved father died in his sleep. Still, Gandhiji had something to look forward to—the birth of his first child. But that was not to be. The joy that Ba and he felt after their child was born lasted just a few days. The baby passed away, leaving the entire family devastated. Gandhiji decided to completely focus on his studies to try and forget the dual tragedies and do something meaningful to make his father proud.

15

The Three Vows

When Gandhiji's high school education ended, he started preparing for college. His family hoped that he would succeed his father as diwan; but times had changed and suitable education was necessary to hold the post. So, a family friend suggested that Gandhiji should go to England to become a barrister. Gandhiji was excited by this possibility, but his mother, Putlibai, was not. She had heard that, in England, young men eat meat, drink liquor and are unfaithful to their wives. She had grave doubts about sending her son to England. What if her naïve son fell under the spell of men of such loose morals? To reassure her mother, before he set off for England, Gandhiji took three solemn vows before a Jain monk who served as a family adviser. He promised that he would never touch wine, women or meat.

By Ship to England

Finances were tight. So, Gandhiji was fortunate that his brother Laxmidas offered to give him a small allowance to help him during his stay in England. Finally, Gandhiji left Bombay (now Mumbai) on board a ship on 4 September 1888. The ship reached Southampton almost four weeks later! Gandhiji left right away for London, which was his final destination in England.

17

Fitting in or Standing out

When Gandhiji first set foot in England, he realized that he did not fit in. He was dressed in a white suit, which he had thought would be perfect for the autumn weather. But it was extremely cold and he found that all the men were dressed in darker coloured suits. Gandhiji didn't speak English very well and he didn't know how to use knives and forks, which made him feel even more alienated. In a desperate attempt to fit in, Gandhiji bought fancy suits, gloves and a top hat—the kind Englishmen wore in those days. He took lessons in violin and dancing. He had to pay through his nose for all these, but even then, he was no more English than when he had started! Finally, Gandhiji gave up. He'd realized that in an attempt to fit in, he was actually trading off the opportunity to stand out.

When Gandhiji Learnt to Cook

When Gandhiji reached England, he found that there weren't a lot of options for a vegetarian. He spent days eating raw, tasteless vegetables that came with the meals he ordered at restaurants and filled himself with bread. He was craving for a good vegetarian meal, and then one day, he found a restaurant called The Central—a heaven for vegetarians. But the restaurant was expensive and he couldn't afford to eat there every day. So, he bought a cooker and learnt to cook his own food. After that, carrot soup became his favourite thing to make!

19

A Vegetarian in London

After Gandhiji discovered The Central and subsequently learnt to cook too, he found it very easy to keep his promise to his mother of not eating meat. He purchased a book titled *A Plea for Vegetarianism and Other Essays* by Henry Stephens Salt, which had a great influence on him. At the restaurant, he met other vegetarians who were members of the Vegetarian Society. They asked him to join them, something that Gandhiji was more than happy to do. Gandhiji even designed a logo for the Vegetarian Society!

Tragedy Strikes Again

Gandhiji studied hard, gave his exams and, at the age of twenty two, became a lawyer on 11 June 1891. He was looking forward to go home, and so, he boarded a ship the very next day, his mind full of hope and longing to see his family after almost three long years. He had a lot of time to think during the long journey back to his homeland. Would he make a good lawyer? What did the future hold for him? Meanwhile, his brother Laxmidas was awaiting his arrival at the dock in Bombay with some terrible news. In his absence, his beloved mother had passed away. Gandhiji was shattered.

25

21

Gandhiji's First Case

Gandhiji decided to practise law in Bombay. The cases were not easy to come by for a novice lawyer. Gandhiji's expenses were mounting every month. About this time, he took up a case of one Mamibai, but the agent who got him the case said that Gandhiji would have to pay a commission to him for bringing the case. Gandhiji emphatically declined but got the case all the same. It was an easy case, not likely to last longer than a day. It was Gandhiji's debut in the court. He appeared for the defendant and had to cross-examine the prosecutor's witnesses. He stood up, but his knees shook. His head started reeling and he could think of no question to ask. He sat down and told the agent that he could not conduct the case, and it would be better for the client to hire some other lawyer. Another lawyer was duly engaged by the agent, for whom, of course, winning the case was a piece of cake.

Wanted, an English Teacher

After the case of Mamibai, Gandhiji thought it wise to not take up any more cases until he was sure he'd be able to conduct them. He decided to take up a teacher's job to make ends meet. His knowledge of the English language was good and he could teach English in some school. Gandhiji came across an advertisement in the papers: WANTED, AN ENGLISH TEACHER TO TEACH ONE HOUR DAILY. SALARY Rs 75. It had been posted by a popular high school. Gandhiji applied for the post and was called for an interview. He went there with high hopes, but when the principal found that he wasn't a graduate, he refused to take him. 'But I have passed the London Matriculation with Latin as my second language,' said Gandhiji. 'True, but we want a graduate,' insisted the principal. Gandhiji was disappointed. He then decided that spending more time in Bombay was of no use. So, he went back to Rajkot.

23

Colonial Arrogance

Gandhiji returned to Rajkot where he prepared legal documents for the economically weaker people and helped them with legal matters. One day, Gandhiji's brother Laxmidas came to him with a problem. He told him that he had been accused of helping one of the heirs to the Porbandar throne to misappropriate jewellery that belonged to the State. He told Gandhiji that the case was being handled by the British political agent, Charles Ollivant. As luck would have it, Gandhiji had made Ollivant's acquaintance in England, so he agreed to speak to him on his brother's behalf. Gandhiji went to Ollivant's residence and reminded him of their meeting in London, but Ollivant was rude and unrelenting. He refused to listen to Gandhiji. To his shock, Gandhiji was shoved out. This humiliating incident left a deep impression on him.

From Rajkot to South Africa

A few months went by. Then, he heard that an Indian businessman, who owned a shipping business in South Africa, was looking for a lawyer. The businessman's name was Dada Abdulla Sheth and he lived in Durban. The fee he was offering was attractive, and so, Gandhiji decided to go, even though that meant leaving his wife and small children behind. In April 1893, Gandhiji set sail once more—this time for South Africa.

25

A Brush with Racism

Gandhiji had no idea of the racial discrimination practised by the regime in South Africa. The moment he landed in South Africa, he noticed people being mean and nasty to Dada Abdulla, who, to Gandhiji's astonishment, didn't seem to mind at all! The Indians were denied their basic human rights, while the whites clung to their racial superiority. With about 1,00,000 members, South Africa's Indian population at that time was substantial. Many Indians had come to the country as labourers who worked for pitiful wages in mines and sugar plantations. Europeans regarded them as inferior and called them 'coolies' or *samis*.

Tale of the Turban

Gandhiji was a qualified barrister, better educated than most of the whites in South Africa, yet his Indian origin put him in a disadvantageous place. This was first brought home to him on his very first day at the court. Gandhiji was wearing a turban. The magistrate looked at him annoyingly and roared, 'Take off your turban, Mr Gandhi.' Gandhiji felt deeply humiliated. He gave the magistrate an icy stare and replied, 'I won't.' He then picked up his files and left the courtroom.

27 Thrown off the Train

In 1893, Gandhiji was travelling from Durban to Pretoria in South Africa by train. He was seated in the first-class compartment when a white man entered. He looked at Gandhiji and snorted in contempt, 'Bloody Indian!' He then summoned the white railway officials. The officials entered the compartment and ordered Gandhiji to shift to the van compartment, since non-whites were not permitted in first-class compartments. Gandhiji thought this unreasonable. 'I have a first-class ticket,' Gandhiji told the officials, 'and I insist on travelling first class.' 'No, you can't,' said one of the officials. 'You must leave the compartment, or else I shall have to call the police to push you out.' Gandhiji was not one to surrender meekly. 'Yes, you may,' he said. 'I refuse to get out voluntarily.' A constable then entered the compartment and pushed him out. His luggage was also thrown out. The train steamed away as Gandhiji watched the tail light melt away in darkness.

A Life-Changing Decision

During the freezing night that Gandhiji spent in the waiting room, a flurry of questions jostled in his mind. Should he fight for his rights? Or should he go back to India? His sense of right and wrong left him with little choice. Gandhiji decided he won't run away. He decided to fight for justice. The following evening, he boarded another train to continue his trip. Its next stop was Charlestown, where passengers disembarked and continued by stagecoach before boarding a train again at Johannesburg. The man in-charge of the coach forced Gandhiji to sit on top of the coach rather than inside it. Then, he tried to make him sit on the footboard under the driver's seat. Gandhiji protested and was beaten up. But Gandhiji didn't give in and, despite these unhappy incidents, reached Pretoria in a first-class train carriage.

29

Johnston's Family Hotel

When Gandhiji reached Pretoria, he gave the ticket to the ticket collector at the exit gate and asked him about a place to stay. The ticket collector did not help Gandhiji, but an African-American man standing nearby offered to help. He took Gandhiji to a small hotel run by an American. It was called Johnston's Family Hotel. The American owner agreed to give Gandhiji a room on one condition—that his food would be served to him in his hotel room. He reasoned that the other guests in the hotel would not like a coloured man to dine with them in the common dining area. But later, the owner found out that the guests did not mind at all and Gandhiji was served food in the common dining area along with other guests.

Footpaths out of Bounds

In Pretoria, South Africa, Gandhiji was once walking besides the home of the President of Transvaal, Peter Kruger. The house seemed unusually modest to him. Suddenly, he was hauled up by an armed guard who almost kicked him off into the street and threatened him with dire consequences if he did not move away immediately. Apparently, according to the rules of Transvaal at that time, coloured people were forbidden to use footpaths and could not move outdoors after 9 p.m. without a permit! Gandhiji was fortunate that a new friend he had made, Michael Coates, happened to pass by on his horse. He stopped the guard and made him apologize to Gandhiji.

31
Gandhiji and Tolstoy

Gandhiji had met Michael Coates through his employer's attorney, Mr Baker. Coates lent Gandhiji many books to read. One of them happened to be *The Kingdom of God Is Within You* by Leo Tolstoy. That was the book that Gandhiji picked up to read on the very same day that he'd had the unpleasant experience with the armed guard in Pretoria. That book left an everlasting impression on him and helped mould his way of thinking. 'Love your enemies' was the greatest lesson he learnt from that book.

A Haircut for Gandhiji

Once in Pretoria, Gandhiji went to an English salon for a haircut. The English barber contemptuously refused to cut the hair of an Indian. Gandhiji felt deeply hurt. He immediately bought a pair of scissors and cut his hair before a mirror. He could succeed in cutting the hair at the front but spoiled the back. His friends in the court shook with laughter.

'What's wrong with your hair, Gandhi? Have rats eaten it?' they asked.

'We do not allow the barbers in our country to serve our untouchable brothers. I got the reward for this in South Africa. It is the punishment for our own sins,' said Gandhiji.

33

Fighting Prejudice

Gandhiji soon began his legal work. At the same time, he set out to combat the anti-Indian prejudice that was prevalent in South Africa. In most territories in South Africa, Indians were not allowed to vote, were not permitted to walk on footpaths or even to go after nine in the evening without a pass. The threat of deportation was also there. So, Gandhiji decided that the best way to start his campaign was to call a meeting of Indians in Pretoria.

First Public Speech

Incidentally, Tyeb Sheth—Gandhiji's employer Dada Abdulla Sheth's cousin—happened to be the person against whom Gandhiji had been employed to fight the lawsuit. When they met, Tyeb's initial suspicion gave way to empathy for the troubles that Gandhiji had gone through since his arrival in South Africa. Initially, Tyeb remarked that all the Indians had learnt to live with the unfairness of their lives. In the course of their discussion, Gandhiji said that the Indians needed to organize themselves to be able to improve their lives there. Tyeb Sheth then offered to organize a meeting at his own home. Gandhiji gave his first public speech at that gathering. When he addressed the group, he found that he was not as tongue-tied as he had been in the Bombay court. On the contrary, he gave a brilliant speech, full of fervour.

35

The Case Is Settled

The lawsuit between cousins Dada Abdulla Sheth and Tyeb Sheth was settled out of court in favour of Gandhiji's employer. But Tyeb Sheth was devastated as he would have to pay up £37,000 as a lump sum. When he came to Gandhiji for help, he offered to speak to his employer and convinced him to allow Tyeb to pay back that large amount in manageable instalments. With that done, Gandhiji was all set to return to India via Durban.

Delayed Departure

When Gandhiji reached Durban on his way back to India, Dada Abdulla Sheth organized a grand farewell for him. At the gathering, Gandhiji found out that the Natal government was planning to introduce a bill that would disallow all Indians from voting. Gandhiji was appalled by this latest move. Many at the gathering suggested that he stay back and help, so Gandhiji said that he would delay his departure by a month, thinking that the matter would be resolved by then.

How wrong he was! On 22 May 1894, the Natal Indian Congress was formed to fight injustice. Gandhiji finally went back to India two whole years later, in 1896, only to bring his family back with him, as his work in South Africa was still incomplete.

37

Short-Lived Stint in India

Back in India, Gandhiji spent his time spreading the word about the conditions of Indians in Africa—he issued a pamphlet to express the same. Since the paper had a green cover, it was called the *Green Pamphlet*. News reporters sent information about the pamphlet to South Africa. Unfortunately, they twisted the information and reported things that were not even written in the pamphlet. This spread rumours in South Africa. Just before a meeting in Calcutta (now Kolkata) where Gandhiji was to deliver a speech, he received a telegram from his old employer, Dada Abdulla Sheth, asking him to return to Durban immediately. This time, his family—Ba and their two sons, Harilal and Manilal—boarded the ship with him.

Eventful Journey

On board the ship to South Africa with his family, Gandhiji insisted that Ba and the boys wore shoes and ate their meals using forks and knives. He wanted them to get used to these habits before the ship reached South Africa. Ba was not happy with these new rules, but she played along. Suddenly, during the voyage, things started falling off tables. Gandhiji reassured his family by saying that it was just temporary bad weather. What started as a minor disturbance at sea soon changed into a terrible storm, with all passengers hurrying to their cabins as quickly as possible. Gandhiji did his best to calm Ba and the children, who had never travelled by ship before. He finally managed to distract them by getting them to watch the beautiful waves of the sea instead of focusing on the storm.

39

Unwelcome

The Gandhi family's arrival in Durban was traumatic, to say the least. There was a mob waiting to beat Gandhiji up. Cries of 'Go home, Gandhi!' and 'Arrest him!' were heard all over the docks. Gandhiji's pamphlet and the bad press surrounding it had made the white rulers furious. They were determined to teach him a lesson. Fortunately, Dada Abdulla Sheth's current lawyer F.A. Laughton came aboard and recommended that Ba and the boys leave the ship separately to ensure their safety. Once that happened, Laughton and Gandhiji also left the ship, but they got spotted. Laughton recommended that they run, but it was of no use. The crowd moved in and started beating and kicking Gandhiji until he fell to the ground. Suddenly, a loud voice was heard over the din of the mob, 'Leave that man alone!' It was the voice of Mrs Alexander, the wife of the police superintendent who happened to be there at the dock. How lucky for Gandhiji! The brave lady held the mob back until the police arrived. Gandhiji was reunited with his family with the help of the police superintendent and his men. But they were far from safe—the mob had followed them!

The Great Escape Artist

The kind superintendent then came up with a plan for Gandhiji to escape in disguise. Gandhiji took shelter in the house of his friend Rustomji. The mob surrounded the house and it kept growing. The police were finding it difficult to control the swelling crowds. Gandhiji was worried about the women and the children in the house and decided to leave at once. The police gave him the uniform of a constable and, in this disguise, he quietly slipped away! When the crowd was told that Gandhiji had, in fact, walked right through them, they just couldn't believe it!

41

A Stint in the Army

Just about a year before the Boer War broke out, the Gandhis had another son, Ramdas. Gandhiji felt that if the Indians expected to be treated as British citizens, they would have to do their bit to support the British troops. And in keeping with his credo of non-violence, he suggested that the Indians serve in the Ambulance Corps. Gandhiji served as a Sergeant Major and saw fierce action in the battle of Spion Kop. He was even awarded a medal by the British for making a significant contribution during the battle.

Medical Successes

In March 1904, the Black Plague had broken out at Brickfields, a poor area in Johannesburg where Indian workers lived. Gandhiji knew he had to help those people as much as he could. Along with his clerks, he briskly cycled to that part of the town. They found that the city council had given a filthy, disused warehouse to be used as the field hospital. Gandhiji and his boys got down to cleaning the place. Patients were dying and Gandhiji wanted to try his earth treatment as a last resort to try and save lives. He was allowed to try it out on three patients. Wet earth packages were tied around the heads and chests of the patients. And to everyone's amazement, the treatment worked! Two of his three patients survived.

43

Gandhiji, the Best Man

Gandhiji's friend Henry Polak wanted to marry a girl called Millie who lived in London. However, he was not sure whether he should marry her, as it would mean that she would have to settle in South Africa. According to Henry's father, Polak senior, Millie was physically weak and might not be able to cope up with the strenuous life in South Africa. When Gandhiji came to know about this, he wrote a letter to Polak senior explaining that the simple life in South Africa would actually be beneficial for her health. He also wrote a letter to Millie and assured her that she would be welcomed in the Polak family. On reading Gandhiji's letter, Millie decided to go to Africa and get married there. Gandhiji was Polak's best man. Since Millie was a Christian and Polak a Jew, the marriage had to be registered. But since Gandhiji was an Indian, the English registrar would not accept him. Polak refused to name anyone else as his best man. Gandhiji then had a talk with the magistrate—a good friend of his—who then readily agreed to register the marriage.

Two Pounds

On one occasion, a young friend of Millie Polak was trying to qualify for a professional examination. She hardly had any money and was going through a rough time. One day, while talking to Gandhiji about her young friend, Millie said, 'She absolutely needs shoes and stockings and does not see the means to get them. Of course, if she can get through this year, she will be able to manage, but it is the immediate present that is the trouble. I wish I had some money to help her.' 'Do not worry about her,' Gandhiji replied. 'She is too fine a character to be hurt by hardships; she will not fail and will manage to get through all right.' A few days later, when Millie met her young friend, she told her, 'I 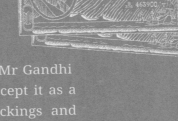 have had such a wonderful surprise! Mr Gandhi sent me two pounds, asking me to accept it as a little present from him.' So the stockings and shoes were taken care of, but Gandhiji never mentioned it to Millie.

45

The Phoenix Farm

One day, Henry Polak gave Gandhiji a book to read. It was *Unto This Last* by John Ruskin. Strongly inspired by this book that encouraged social equality and simple living, Gandhiji bought a farm close to Phoenix Station in 1904. Ba joined him soon with their four boys—the youngest one, Devdas, was born in 1900. Gandhiji also invited Polak to live on the farm. Here, they washed and cleaned themselves and even the toilets. They grew their own food. The idea was to live simply and be self-sufficient with everyone drawing the same wages. Gandhiji decided that the newspaper *Indian Opinion*, which he was financing and writing a piece for regularly, would be run from the farm too.

The Football Lover

Believe it or not, Gandhiji was a huge football buff! Although he never played the game professionally, he was a great football aficionado. During his stay in South Africa, Gandhiji formed two football clubs—one in Johannesburg and the other in Pretoria. They were both named the Passive Resisters—inspired by the political philosophy in the writings of Henry Thoreau and Leo Tolstoy.

47

A Promise Is a Promise

There was a time when Gandhiji was practising law in the city of Johannesburg in South Africa. His office was about five kilometres from his house. One day, Henry Polak asked Gandhiji's thirteen-year-old son, Manilal, to get a book from the office. But Manilal completely forgot about this until Polak reminded him that evening. Gandhiji heard about it and called Manilal. 'I know it's dark and the way is long, but you gave your word to Mr Polak. You promised him to get his book. Go and get it now.' Kasturba, Gandhiji's wife, was very upset when she heard of this—the punishment seemed far too severe for forgetting to get a book; it could, of course, be brought the next day. But no one had the courage to say anything. Gandhiji's close aide, Kalyan Bhai, offered to fetch the book, but Gandhiji refused by saying, 'The promise was made by Manilal not you.' 'Very well,' said Kalyan Bhai, 'Manilal will fetch the book, but let me go with him.' Gandhiji agreed to this. Manilal and Kalyan Bhai then delivered the book to Polak in the late night hour.

Tooth Trouble

In 1906, Gandhiji was in London, fighting the cause of the Indians in South Africa with the British statesmen. One day, Gandhiji developed a severe toothache. He was busy in a South Africa committee meeting when his friend Dr Joshia Oldfield called on him. Coming out from the committee meeting, Gandhiji asked the doctor if he could take out the tooth that was troubling him. The doctor examined his mouth and found the cause of the pain. 'Why don't you visit a dentist?' he suggested. 'I don't have the time,' said Gandhiji. 'If you take the tooth out for me here and now, I will be very grateful—it's disturbing my concentration.' The doctor went out, bought a pair of forceps and came back. Gandhiji asked the committee to excuse him for a minute. He came to his room where the doctor was waiting and without a sigh or a murmur bore the painful extraction of his tooth. After it was done, Gandhiji thanked the doctor gently and went back to the meeting.

49

The Black Act

A new government bill called the Black Act required all Asians over eight years of age to be fingerprinted and registered with the authorities. Gandhiji called for a meeting at the Empire Theatre in Johannesburg for all Indians to figure out what to do. Gandhiji called for a passive resistance movement, which would be non-violent, to register their protest. He felt, like many Indians did, that fingerprinting was meant only for criminals. The registration offices were surrounded by supporters of this movement. 'No to Black Act', 'No to Registration' and 'We Are Not Criminals' read some of the placards. When Gandhiji discussed the need for a name for this movement, Gandhiji's cousin, Maganlal, suggested *sadagraha*. Gandhiji nodded, but said he preferred the name Satyagraha, meaning 'a force born of truth'. Thus, the Satyagraha movement was born.

To Jail

By the end of 1907, out of the 13,000 Indians living in South Africa, only 511 had registered themselves under the Black Act. It was a victory for the Satyagraha movement for sure, but in January 1908, Gandhiji was called to court and sentenced to imprisonment for two months. But very soon, over 150 Indians and Satyagrahis joined him in jail. One day, while in jail, Gandhiji was told that Jan Christian Smuts, the colonel secretary of the Transvaal government, wanted to talk to him. He was taken to Pretoria to meet Smuts, who was looking for a way to save the government any more 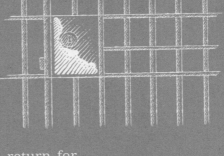 embarrassment. He suggested that in return for the Indians registering themselves, he would do all he could to have the Black Act withdrawn. Gandhiji agreed to meet his fellow Indians with his proposal. He was free to go.

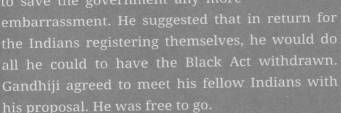

51

Rebel in the Ranks

Not everybody was happy when Gandhiji spoke to a large group of Indians regarding the proposal made by the Colonel Secretary Jan Christian Smuts. Mir Alam, who had once been a client of Gandhiji, was one of them. He vowed to kill anyone who did get registered. So, when Gandhiji led a group of Indians to the registration office, he was stopped and warned by Mir Alam. When Gandhiji decided to carry on, he was hit in the head causing him to fall unconscious. His friends rushed him to the safety of the home of Joseph Doke, a Baptist priest and one of Gandhiji's friends. To keep his end of the agreement, Gandhiji insisted on signing the papers while he was still recovering. But by May 1908, even though thousands had followed Gandhiji's lead, the government had done nothing to repel the Black Act. So, as a mark of protest, thousands followed Gandhiji in burning their registration papers.

A New Car

When Gandhiji was being released from jail after having served his sentence for the Satyagraha struggle, he saw his friend Hermann Kallenbach at the prison gates. He was standing next to a shining new car that he had bought to take Gandhiji home. Gandhiji resolutely refused to sit in the car. 'It is foolish to spend so much money on a car when other people are suffering. You must return it to the seller before doing anything else,' Gandhiji said.

On another occasion, Kallenbach and Gandhiji were returning to South Africa from England by ship. Kallenbach had an expensive pair of binoculars. Gandhiji looked at it and commented that one should only keep the things that are absolutely essential. The binoculars were expensive but not essential. Persuaded by Gandhiji, Kallenbach threw them into the sea.

53

No Pistol Can Save Me

Once in South Africa, Gandhiji was going for a meeting. Hermann Kallenbach was to accompany him. Kallenbach had heard that the whites were planning to attack Gandhiji, so he quietly slipped a revolver into his pocket. When Gandhiji got to know about this, he was greatly annoyed. 'Is your trust placed in God or in this revolver?' he asked Kallenbach. 'There's no need for you to come with me,' he told his friend. 'I need no protection. No pistol can save me, only God can. As long as he desires to make use of me, he is bound to keep me safe.'

Tolstoy Farm—A Gift

Gandhiji's friend Hermann Kallenbach bought a farm about thirty-three kilometres from Johannesburg and donated it to the Satyagrahi cause because he really believed in what Gandhiji was doing. The farm was named after one of Gandhiji's favourite authors, Leo Tolstoy. Kallenbach and Gandhiji would often walk to Johannesburg and back. They had a lot of time to talk about multifaith prayer meetings, politics, diets, etc. On one such day, Gandhiji brought up the topic of food, stating that he wanted to be in a position to eat just to survive, not for pleasure. But when they reached the farm, Gandhiji's fourth son, Devdas, was enjoying a candy bar! To everyone's shock, Gandhiji started hitting himself in remorse and said that he would fast for a week to make up for his son's behaviour. Poor Devdas promised to never repeat what he had done.

55

Gandhi and Gokhale

On Gandhiji's visit to India from South Africa in 1896, he met the Congress leader Gopal Krishna Gokhale. Gandhiji was deeply impressed with his dedication to his motherland and ideals of public service. Gokhale became Gandhiji's political mentor and guide. When Gokhale visited Gandhiji in South Africa in 1912, Gandhiji took it upon himself to take care of his friend. He cleaned his room, washed and ironed his clothes and cooked his food. Gokhale had with him a scarf, which was a gift from Mahadev Govind Ranade. He treasured the memento with utmost care. On one occasion, the Indians in South Africa hosted a banquet in honour of Gokhale. The scarf was creased and needed ironing. As there was no time to give it to the laundry, Gandhiji offered to iron it. 'I can trust you in the capacity of a lawyer,' said Gokhale, 'but not as a washerman. What if you soil it?' But when Gandhiji ironed the scarf to Gokhale's satisfaction, Gandhiji said, 'I have won your certification. After that, I don't mind if the rest of the world refuses me a certificate.'

60

Defeating a Satyagrahi

On one occasion, Gokhale was unwell, so Gandhiji put him on a strict diet. Gokhale protested against this, but Gandhiji was not to be budged. He continued serving his friend light food such as fruits and boiled vegetables. Gandhiji was so strict that when they were invited over by some friends for dinner, Gandhiji declared that Gokhale could not eat anything there. On the night of the dinner, Gokhale stubbornly refused to leave the house until Gandhiji gave him the permission to eat what he wanted. Gandhiji had to give in. Gokhale laughed and said that he'd defeated a Satyagrahi by going on Satyagraha!

57

The £3 Tax

In 1912, when Gopal Krishna Gokhale visited South Africa, he met General Jan Smuts and was convinced that a settlement was likely to happen in the next few days. But Gandhiji was sceptical. His apprehension proved right when the talks on the Black Act failed and a fresh issue came to light—the Supreme Court in March 1913 ruled that all marriages not performed according to Christian rites were illegal. This was a terrible slur on the honour of Hindu, Muslim and Parsi women and also deprived their children of inheritance. At the same time, the Natal government began to prosecute those Indians in criminal courts who could not pay the annual tax of £3 each. Gandhiji decided to make the legal recognition of Indian marriages and abolition of tax another aim of his Satyagraha.

Ba's Involvement

When the government declared that only Christian marriages would be recognized in South Africa and that the indentured workers from India would have to either sign up for another period of hard labour or pay an annual tax to continue staying in the country, Gandhiji spoke to Ba about getting more actively involved. Apprehensive at first, she soon got her friends to participate in the cause, and in October 1913, they started convincing miners to go on strike to protest. Her efforts quickly bore fruit; within two weeks, more than 5,000 workers went on strike! Of course, the authorities arrested her and sentenced her to three months of hard labour.

59

Jail Yet Again

Gandhiji wanted to help the Indian workers. When their shelters were taken away from them, he asked the workers to follow him to Tolstoy Farm. Over 2,000 workers followed Gandhiji across the Transvaal border. Just about eighty kilometres from Johannesburg, the crowd was stopped and Gandhiji was arrested. When Henry Polak protested, Gandhiji asked all the others to stay calm, stick to their non-violent commitment and follow Polak. He was sentenced to nine months in jail, during which almost 60,000 workers from the railways, plantations, etc. went on strike!

Prisoner No. 1739

In November 1913, Gandhiji was imprisoned by the South African government. He was lodged in Bloemfontein Gaol. Here are some details from his jail card.

No.: 1739

Name: Mohandas Karamchand Gandhi

Religion: Hindu

Age: 43

Trade: Solicitor

Date of Sentence: 11/11/'13

Date of Discharge: 10/11/'14

Sentence: £20 or 3 months (on each of four counts)

Allowed vegetable diet owing to religious scruples.

Diet: 12 bananas, 12 dates, 3 tomatoes and 1 lemon-each, 2 ounces of olive oil and 3 selected groundnuts

61

A Job Well Done

When thousands of Indian workers from all walks of life went on strike in South Africa, the government desperately sought to put a stop to it. So, they resorted to violence, disrupting peaceful protests with force. News about the brutality spread around the world, drawing much public criticism against the local government. It was again time for negotiations. So, Gandhiji's time in jail was cut short and he was called in. When Gandhiji voiced his scepticism to General Jan Smuts, he finally conceded that non-Christian marriages will be recognized, the Satyagrahis in jail will be released and the tax on the indentured workers will be repealed. An agreement to that effect was signed in June 1914. And then, finally, Gandhiji decided to return to India for good. There were many farewell talks and events before he left, attended by the thousands of grateful Indians in South Africa.

Moral Dilemma

Gandhiji felt that his work in South Africa was done and it was now time to return to India. To think that he had originally set out to stay for only one year and ended up staying for more than seven! There were a lot of farewell parties during which Kasturba received several pieces of jewellery as gestures of gratitude for the work done by the Gandhis. She was thrilled with all the gifts, but Gandhiji felt uneasy. He thought about it a lot and felt that the money spent on the jewellery would be better spent on the economically weaker people. So, he asked Ba to return the gifts. Can you imagine her surprise? She refused, saying that she would keep the jewellery to give to her daughters-in-law. But Gandhiji was adamant. They argued a lot, and finally, Ba agreed to give up the gifts to be put in a trust for the whole Indian community.

63

Farewell to South Africa

On 18 July 1914, when Gandhiji was leaving South Africa for good, he gave a farewell speech before his departure. He said that he could not claim any credit for the Indian Relief Act—an Act that abolished the extra tax on Indians, recognized the validity of Hindu and Muslim marriages and allowed free entry for educated Indians into South Africa. He added that it was rather due to the women, the children and the young people who died for the cause and to those who quickened the conscience of South Africa. He ended it by saying, 'I go away with no ill will against a single European.'

From South Africa to England

For the very last time, Gandhiji left South Africa, never to return. His work there was done. While the ship was still at sea, World War I started. In London, Gandhiji met his old friend Gopal Krishna Gokhale who was recouping there. Gokhale congratulated Gandhiji on his work in South Africa and the successes achieved through non-violence and passive resistance. They discussed the power of Satyagraha and how what happened in South Africa was proof of its ability to make a difference. When Gandhiji voiced his eagerness to try the same when he returned to India, Gokhale cautioned him to wait for a while and travel to India to find out first-hand what the present needs of the people living there were.

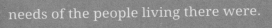

From England to India

In December 1914, Gandhiji and Ba set sail for Bombay, arriving there at the beginning of the New Year. During the journey, Gandhiji and Ba had had time to discuss their hopes and aspirations for their future work in India. Gandhiji was adamant that he would focus on helping the poorer sections of the country. At the Bombay port, they spotted a large crowd. All of them had come to greet Gandhiji, carrying hope and admiration. Gandhi was already well known in India by then because of his fight for the better treatment of Indians in South Africa. He had corresponded regularly with his mentor Gopal Krishna Gokhale and the Indian National Congress. The press was eager to know what he had in mind, now that he was back in India. Gandhiji calmly let them know that he was only going to observe and learn for a while. He was definitely taking his friend Gokhale's advice seriously. The British rulers must have been quite relieved to know that!

Jinnah's Reception

There were many receptions that were organized to welcome Gandhiji when he returned to India. One such reception was held by Mohammed Ali Jinnah of the Indian National Congress and the Muslim League. He had invited many powerful and wealthy men to meet Gandhiji. Everyone was talking about his work in South Africa. Gandhiji had changed from his British suit to a typical Indian outfit on the ship itself. He wanted to feel one with the masses from day one.

67

An Indian in India

On Gopal Krishna Gokhale's urging, Gandhiji decided to travel throughout India to understand the conditions of his fellow countrymen. Having fought to travel first class in South Africa, he now travelled third class with economically weaker Indians, covering the length and breadth of the country. To connect better with the masses, he learnt other languages, such as Bengali and Urdu. As a student of law in England, he'd bought the best of clothes to stay in tune with the fashion of the time. During his stay in South Africa though, he'd realized that Asians and Africans needed to stop imitating Europeans at once. So, when he was in India, his western clothes gave way to his native Kathiawari dress: dhoti, kurta and a turban.

Clothes Make the Man

After he returned to India in 1915, he went on an extensive tour of India, during which he came to realize what poverty meant. Once, in Madurai, after addressing a large public gathering, the visuals of those half-clad men and women in the audience filled his thoughts that night. The next morning, when Mr Rajan—who was translating Gandhiji's English speeches into Tamil —came to fetch him, he found Gandhiji in a loin cloth. 'It is time for the meeting. Please get ready soon,' he said. 'I'm ready,' replied Gandhiji. Surprised, Mr Rajan asked again, 'Are you not planning to get dressed for the gathering? To which Gandhi said, 'From today onwards, this is what I am going to wear—the dress that every Indian wears.'

Satyagraha Ashram

In May 1915, with funds from supporters and friends, the Satyagraha Ashram was set up. The idea was that life in the ashram would serve as a model and inspiration to Indians all over the country. Everyone ate together and tried to live as one big family. Living a simple life filled with love, non-violence and truth, every occupant was expected to do everything in their power in the fight against untouchability. Once, when an untouchable family wanted to join the ashram and Gandhiji agreed, his cousin Maganlal's wife, Santok, threatened to fast in protest. Gandhiji said he too would fast to protest against her fast! Ba was not happy either, but both Santok and she soon came around and accepted the new family into the ashram.

An Altruist in the Ashram

Though Gandhiji had allowed the Dalit family to live in the ashram, the prejudice ran so deep in the minds of people that many patrons of the ashram withdrew their support. Soon, the money began to dry up. Gandhiji was wondering how to sustain the ashram when, one day, a young man, a seth, drove up to the gate of the ashram in a fancy car, handed a bag of money to Gandhiji and drove off. Inside the bag was Rs 13,000—a huge sum at that time. Later, Gandhiji discovered that this man was Ambalal Sarabhai, a mill owner. A few years after this incident, Gandhiji led a strike by workers at a textile mill in Ahmedabad and among its owners was the same Ambalal Sarabhai.

71

The Stains of Indigo

In 1917, Gandhiji visited Champaran in Bihar where the European cultivators were forcing peasants to grow indigo instead of food crops in order to maximize their profits. Gandhiji surveyed the area to understand the situation, recorded the peasants' sufferings and defied the British order to leave the place, deciding to get arrested instead. Eventually, the government stopped the compulsory cultivation of indigo and paid compensation to the peasants.

An Impression Forever

It's said that when people met Gandhiji once, they remembered him forever! Vallabhbhai Patel was a successful lawyer. He was once playing bridge at the Ahmedabad Club when a man, wearing a weather-worn dhoti and looking like a farmer, came to his table and invited him and his friends to come and listen to his speech. Patel was not at all interested and went back to his cards. But something about this dhoti-clad man made him curious. So he went to listen to him. When he heard Gandhiji speaking, he was immediately converted to the cause of Satyagraha. He gave up his law practice, stopped wearing western clothes and worked with Gandhiji for the rest of his life. Many years later, when Gandhiji and Vallabhbhai Patel were both in the Yerwada Jail for participating in the Satyagraha movement, Patel even taught Gandhiji how to play bridge.

The Kheda Satyagraha

In 1918, a famine was imminent in the Kheda district of Gujarat. The peasants were plagued by poverty and scant resources. But even then, the British government wanted to increase their taxes—they said that if the taxes were not paid, the property of the peasants would be seized. Gandhiji, along with Vallabhbhai Patel, organized a major tax revolt. The peasants of Kheda signed a petition and called for the tax to be scrapped. Even when their lands were confiscated and they were arrested, they stood their ground and refused to pay up, forcing the government to withdraw the tax and return their properties. That's when people started calling Gandhiji 'Bapu' and 'the Father of the Nation'. In his autobiography, *The Story of My Experiments with Truth*, this is what Gandhiji writes about the Kheda Satyagraha: 'The Kheda Satyagraha marks the beginning of an awakening among the peasants of Gujarat, the beginning of their true political education'.

First Hunger Strike

In 1918, millworkers in Ahmedabad launched a protest against the mill owners, asking for a substantial increase in their salaries. Gandhiji felt that their struggle was a just one. So, he advised the workers to go on a non-violent strike. Although mill workers initially took part in the strike, they started returning to work after around a week. Gandhiji became alone—the people he was fighting for left him behind and went to work. He learnt the biggest lesson of his life that common people cannot fight forever. To help the workers, Gandhiji went on his first political fast in India, pledging not to eat until the mill owners gave in. It was a successful campaign and won the workers a thirty-five per cent raise in their wages.

75

All-India Train Tour

While many things seemed quite easy and possible at the planning stage, travelling third class around the country was actually very difficult. Gandhiji found this out first-hand, even if the experience was most instructive. At Bolpur, the younger Gandhi boys who had travelled with some friends from South Africa to Shantiniketan were waiting for their parents' arrival. Rabindranath Tagore was there to meet and interact with Gandhiji. It gave Gandhiji great pleasure to interact with one of the best intellectuals in the country. The feeling must have been mutual. Many from around the country, who wanted to meet Gandhiji, would travel to Shantiniketan. Tagore would introduce Gandhiji to the crowd gathered around as the Mahatma—an apt title that he remained embarrassed about forever.

A Poet's Present

The poet Rabindranath Tagore gave the title Mahatma to Gandhiji. Here, Tagore explains why: 'He (Gandhi) stopped at the thresholds of the huts of the thousands of dispossessed, dressed like one of their own. He spoke to them in their own language. Here was living truth at last, and not only quotations from books. For this reason the "Mahatma", the name given to him by the people of India, is his real name. Who else has felt like him that all Indians are his own flesh and blood? At Gandhi's call, India blossomed forth to new greatness . . .'

77

WWI Recruitment Failure

Gandhiji was of the strong belief that for Swaraj (self-rule) to work, Hindus and Muslims needed to be united. So, when two prominent Muslim leaders were in custody, he asked the viceroy of India Lord Chelmsford to release them in the name of friendship. A prominent member of the legislative council protested and asked Gandhiji to prove his friendship by conducting a recruitment drive first. Gandhiji, who expected thousands to join the British to fight during World War I, was hurt and taken aback when hardly any did, in spite of him travelling all over the country in the summer of 1918. Then, in sheer exhaustion, he collapsed into defeat. Fortunately, the war came to an end while he was recovering, but Gandhiji felt highly demoralized by then.

All-India Hartal

The Rowlatt Act was aimed at keeping the Indian population under control and supposedly curbing unrest, but it also meant that anyone could be arrested for suspected political activities without a trial or appeal. Even someone caught carrying a pamphlet that appeared to be critical of the government could get two years in jail. Gandhiji's answer to the much-hated Act was an all-India hartal. Delhi went on strike on 30 March 1919 with the rest of the country following on 6 April 1919. Civil disobedience was what he urged everyone to follow with no damage to be caused to anyone or any property. From the point of public involvement, it was a huge success. Shops big and small remained closed, as did businesses.

Violent Aftermath

The initial success and peacefulness of the civil disobedience in protest over the Rowlatt Act was short-lived. Trouble started in Punjab. In the hope of calming things down, Gandhiji travelled there, but he was ordered to go back to Bombay on the assumption that more trouble would erupt with his presence. Somehow, a rumour that Gandhiji had been arrested spread around the country. Violence broke out everywhere; mobs were angry. In Ahmedabad, a train station and other buildings were set on fire; in Amritsar, three men were killed . . . Gandhiji was distraught. He had misread the people. He immediately stopped the Satyagraha. He realized that he had made a grave mistake; people were not yet ready for Satyagraha.

Boycott of Foreign Cloth

The hard line of the British Raj made more and more imminent people eager to support Gandhiji and his Satyagraha movement—Motilal Nehru and his son, Jawaharlal, to name a few. Motilal was a well-known member of Congress at the time, and he asked how they could help. Gandhiji suggested that he obtain the support of Congress to boycott the use of foreign cloth and switch to khadi instead. Gandhiji explained how this gesture would create employment in the villages and that the cloth would introduce the practice of hand-spinning and hand-weaving in India. To put this into action, a ceremonial fire was lit at Motilal Nehru's home. Many people, including other members of Congress, were present for the symbolic burning of the foreign cloth. And so, it came to be that the Nehrus and many other Congress members started wearing clothes made of khadi.

The Tale of the Torn Dhoti

Once, Gandhiji was touring Tamil Nadu by train. As his train chugged into the town of Virudhnagar where he had to get off, he got up from a nap and stood up. This strained the dhoti around his waist and caused it to tear a little. On seeing Gandhiji's torn dhoti, the man accompanying him said, 'Bapu, your dhoti is torn. You hardly have a minute to change; we've almost reached the station!' 'Why change?' asked Gandhiji, as he immediately went to the washroom and adjusted his dhoti a little. He came back a moment later and politely asked the same person, 'See now, do you see any tear? Actually, there is a lot of it left to get torn!'

Gandhiji and His Spinning Wheel

Gandhiji spent some time every day spinning yarn on his charkha. This was his way of spreading the message to his countrymen to value manual labour and self-reliance. Gandhiji saw spinning yarn as an important means of earning a livelihood for the poor. Soon, the charkha became a symbol of India's freedom struggle.

83

A Kurta for Gandhiji

Once, in a gathering, a little boy approached Gandhiji. He was distressed to see the way Gandhiji was dressed. Such a great man, yet he didn't even wear a shirt, the boy wondered. 'Why don't you wear a kurta?' he questioned Gandhiji. 'Where's the money, child?' Gandhiji asked him gently. 'I'm very poor and I can't afford a kurta,' he went on to add. The boy's heart was filled with pity. 'My mother makes all my clothes. I will ask her to sew a kurta for you,' he said. 'How many kurtas can your mother make?' Gandhiji asked. 'As many as you need,' came the reply. 'One, two, three . . .' Gandhiji muttered for a moment and said, 'But I'm not alone, child. I have a large family. And it wouldn't be right for me to be the only one to wear a kurta.' 'Just how many kurtas do you need?' insisted the child. 'I have forty crore brothers and sisters,' Gandhiji explained. 'Till every one of them has a kurta, how can I wear one? Tell me, can your mother make kurtas for all of them?' The boy became thoughtful at this question. But Gandhiji was right. The whole nation was his family and he was their father.

Bapu on a Bicycle

Apart from the spinning wheel, the wheels of his bicycle were another important part of Gandhiji's life. When Gandhiji was in South Africa, he protested against a law that discriminated against people cycling on the streets. It required every native to hold a cycle permit for riding a cycle in the municipal area and to wear a numbered badge on his arm. Gandhiji found this idea ridiculous and fought against it. He commuted to work by bicycle—a distance of six miles from his home.

In 1904, when there was an outbreak of plague in Johannesburg's 'coolie location'—where quarters were assigned to the coolies—Gandhiji rushed to the spot on a bicycle and helped the doctors by attending to the patients. When he moved to Ahmedabad in 1915, he rode the bicycle from Gujarat Vidyapith to Sabarmati Ashram whenever he would be late for his evening prayers.

85

A Weekly Day of Silence

Gandhiji became the leader of the Congress party. He toured all over the country to explain and promote the possibility of Swaraj. This took a toll on him and he found himself exhausted all the time, even sleeping on the floor of his office sometimes. And so, he decided to take a page out of the Trappist monks' way of living, those that he had encountered in South Africa who propagated silence. Gandhiji started keeping a day of silence every week, during which he would only talk in case of an emergency; otherwise, written notes sufficed.

A Child's Gift

One day, Kaka Kalelkar, a social reformer and Gandhiji's aide, found him anxiously searching his desk.

'What are you looking for?' Kakasaheb asked.

'I've lost my pencil,' Gandhiji answered.

So, Kakasaheb took out his pencil and offered it to him.

'No, no, I want my own pencil,' Gandhiji insisted.

'Okay, use this for the time being,' said Kakasaheb. 'I'll find your pencil later.'

'You don't understand. That pencil is very precious to me,' Gandhiji said. 'Natesan's little son gave it to me in Madras. He gave it with so much love and affection. I cannot bear to lose it.'

So, Kakasaheb joined Gandhiji in the search and they found it—a tiny piece, barely two inches long. But it made Gandhiji so happy! To him, it was no ordinary pencil. It was the token of a child's love, which was so very precious.

87

Beyond Agile

In 1921, Gandhiji was attending the All India Congress Committee session in Vijayawada, Andhra Pradesh. After the session, there was a meeting for which people gathered in huge numbers. A dais was erected on a raised mound and the wooden pillars on the dais held up the canopy. Gandhiji was on the dais and he started the meeting. Suddenly, a cow got into the crowd. There was a stampede and people began to rush towards the dais. It was impossible to control the crowd. With people trying to climb on to the mound, it looked as though the wooden pillars would collapse and Gandhiji would get crushed under the canopy. All of a sudden, Gandhiji jumped on a chair and eyed the crowds that were thronging the dais from all sides. He jumped from chair to chair, got down where he could see the crowd was the thinnest and jostled his way to safety. He then stopped a passing vehicle and got to the place where he was staying. When his associates came back, they were surprised to see Gandhiji in his room, calmly answering the letters that were awaiting a response.

Scorpion Bite

In March 1922, Gandhiji was sentenced to six years' jail for writing three articles in *Young India*, a weekly paper published by him. He was taken to Yerwada Jail where he spent his time spinning and reading. He had been allowed to take in his charkha, the Gita, the Bible, the Koran and a book of prayer songs. A large African prisoner was appointed as his attendant. One day, there was a sudden commotion. The attendant was bitten by a scorpion in Gandhiji's cell! Gandhiji quickly asked the guard for a knife, knowing that the venom had to be taken out as soon as possible. But the guard's knife was dirty, so Gandhiji immediately started to suck the venom out and spat it out. His attendant's life was saved.

The Gandhian Austerity

When Gandhiji was arrested and put in the Yerwada Jail in 1930, the government had fixed a sum of Rs 150 as his monthly allowance. On the first day, the English superintendent of the jail, Major Martin, came to meet Gandhiji. He bought along a lot of furniture, crockery and cooking utensils for him. Gandhiji asked him to take everything away. The major thought Gandhiji was dissatisfied with what he had brought. He tried to pacify Gandhiji by saying, 'I have written to the government, asking them to increase the allowance of an honoured guest such as you to at least Rs 300 a month. I have every hope the government will agree.' Gandhiji saw that the major had not understood him. So, he explained, 'That is all good. But after all, the money would come from the Indian Treasury, would it not? I do not want to increase the burden on my country. I hope that my boarding expenses will not come to more than Rs 35 a month.' And so, all the furniture and crockery were sent away.

Dattoba's Limping

At Yerwada Jail, a prisoner named Dattoba was assigned the duty of cooking food for Gandhiji. The fellow was suffering from arthritis and had a limp while walking. He was assigned jobs like heating water for Gandhiji, folding his clothes, warming milk for him, etc. Gandhiji noticed him limping. The next morning, he asked the jail superintendent, Major Martin, to permit him to try a naturopathic treatment on Dattoba. Major Martin said he had no objection. 'I will let him keep fast for a few days. Then I will put him on a strict regimen.' Gandhiji would ask Dattoba to see him every day. He would change his diet according to the changes in his condition. In a few days, he was completely cured. No wonder Dattoba started serving Gandhiji with more reverence.

91

A British Nurse's Taunt

In 1924, after almost two years in jail, one day, Gandhiji suddenly developed a severe stomach ache and was rushed to Sassoon Hospital, where it was diagnosed that he had appendicitis and would need an operation. But just before the surgery was to be performed, there was a power cut! It was too late to stop the procedure, so Gandhiji's appendix was removed under torchlight! During his recovery period, he was informed that he would be released from his jail sentence on medical grounds. While he was leaving the hospital, one of the nurses asked him how he felt about being operated upon by a British doctor and treated with British medicine when he had pledged to give up all things British. Gandhiji smiled and explained to her that he had asked for a boycott of all foreign cloth only so that the poor villagers could gain employment.

The Five Virtues

In his public speeches, Gandhiji often gave simple examples to make people understand what he was saying. His biographer Louis Fischer writes: 'During some speeches, he would lift his left hand and open up the five fingers. Taking the first finger between the two fingers of his right hand, he would shake it and say, "This is equality for untouchables", and even those who could not hear him would ask for and get an explanation later from those who had. Then the second finger, "This is spinning". The third finger was sobriety—no alcohol, no opium. The fourth was Hindu-Muslim friendship. The fifth was equality for women. The hand was bound to the body with the wrist. The wrist was non-violence. The five virtues, through non-violence, would free the body of each one of them and hence India.'

93

The Charkha Sangh

In 1925, Gandhiji set up a Charkha Sangh with 50,000 functional charkhas and spinners from 1,500 villages. The manufacturing of spindles and charkhas provided work to village carpenters. The charkha became the giver of employment to the people, which filled hungry stomachs. In the next five years, production and sale of khadi increased and more than 1,00,000 spinners were employed. Gandhiji said, 'I see nothing in the world that can compete with this mill in miniature. Show me another industry or corporation that has—in the course of eighteen years—put four crores of rupees in the pocket of lakhs of the neediest men and women with the same capital expenditure that the Charkha Sangh has done.'

A Copper Coin

Gandhiji travelled to different cities and villages to collect funds for the Charkha Sangh. Once at a meeting in Orissa (now Odisha), after his speech ended, an impoverished, old woman stood up to approach Gandhiji. Her clothes were torn in many places. She jostled by the volunteers to where Gandhiji was seated and touched his feet. Then, she removed one copper coin from the folds of her sari and placed it near his feet. Gandhiji picked it up and put it aside. Jamnalal Bajaj, who was in charge of the Charkha Sangh funds, asked Gandhiji for the coin, but Gandhiji refused. 'I keep cheques worth thousands of rupees for the Charkha Sangh,' Jamnalal Bajaj said laughingly, 'yet you won't trust me with a single copper coin.' 'This copper coin is worth much more than those thousands,' Gandhiji said. 'If a man has several lakhs and he gives away a thousand or two, it doesn't mean much. But this coin was, perhaps, all that the poor woman possessed. What a great sacrifice she made!'

A Cure for Sleeplessness

In 1927, the Indian National Congress and the Indian Trade Union Congress were holding their annual conference in Madras. One of the attendees was Fenner Brockway, a well-known friend of Gandhiji and a delegate of the Independent Labour Party of the UK. But unfortunately, just before the conference, he met with a car accident. When Gandhiji came to know about this, he immediately went to meet Brockway in the hospital, which he continued doing every day even when the Congress was in session and he was hard-pressed for time. On one such day, when Gandhiji went to the hospital, he found that Brockway wasn't too well. It was Gandhiji's day of silence, so he made enquiries by jotting down questions on a piece of paper. Brockway told him that he has not been sleeping at all because of the pain. Then, Brockway reports, 'Gandhi took my hand, and an extraordinary calm came over me. That night, I slept without a drug for the first time.'

A Lesson in Empathy

Mahadev Desai, Gandhiji's secretary was once touring north India with him. One day, he had so much work to finish that he worked through the night and went to sleep only in the early hours of the morning. Desai, therefore, could not get up at the usual hour. When he got up, he saw his morning tea laid out before him. Gandhiji himself did not drink tea, but he knew that Desai could not do without it. So, he went to a nearby restaurant, got tea, milk, sugar, bread and butter, laid it out on the table and waited for Desai to wake up.

97   The Dandi March

During the 1930s, the government controlled the making and selling of salt and asked everyone to pay a Salt Tax. Gandhiji felt that such a tax was unfair and commented that the government would next put a tax on water. The laws were so stringent that a person could be fined even for picking up a handful of sea salt lying on the sand. So, this is exactly what Gandhiji decided to do—pick up salt from the seashore at Dandi . . . and thus was born the Salt March, also regarded as the Dandi March. Gandhiji, along with his seventy-eight companions, walked from Sabarmati Ashram in Ahmedabad to the seashore at Dandi, covering a distance of 400 kilometres. This non-violent movement began on 12 March 1930 and ended on 6 April 1930. Gandhiji and his companions walked up to 24 kilometres every day for twenty-five days to cover the entire distance. Gandhiji was sixty at that time and the oldest among the marchers.

Meals During the March

Gandhiji was highly efficient at organizing things. When he was planning the Dandi March, he sent letters to all the villages en route where the marchers were to stop for food and rest. He also made a list of dishes that were to be served to the marchers.

Morning before departure: *Raab* (a sweet soup made of wheat flour, jaggery, cinnamon, cloves and dried ginger powder) and *dhebra* (thick chapattis made of multigrain flour and flavoured with fenugreek)

Midday: *Bhakri* (thick chapattis flavoured with cumin seeds) and milk or buttermilk

Evening: Roasted gram and puffed rice

Night: Khichri with vegetables and milk or buttermilk

Churchill and Gandhiji

Alas, Gandhiji was put in jail again for violating the Salt Law. He was released for negotiations as things had gone too far and the whole world was condemning the brutal manner in which the British Raj was handling the Indians who were protesting non-violently. Winston Churchill was a staunch critic of Gandhiji. When he heard that the Viceroy Lord Irwin would be negotiating with Gandhiji and other leaders, he could not understand why the British Raj had to appease him. The negotiations went well. All those who were arrested during the unrest earlier were to be released, people who were living along the coast were to be allowed to make their own salt and the non-violent protests would be allowed. Gandhiji was then invited to London to take part in the Second Round Table Conference to discuss the future of India. So, he travelled around Britain and met the poor people who were suffering under the Depression. With the exception of Churchill, he met George Bernard Shaw, Charlie Chaplin and Jan Smuts.

When Gandhiji Met Chaplin

During Gandhiji's 1931 visit to England, the renowned English comic actor, filmmaker and composer Charlie Chaplin wrote to Gandhiji, requesting him for a meeting. But the people around the Mahatma had to tell him who Charlie Chaplin was, as he had no idea! 'He's a famous actor, Bapu,' said one of Gandhiji's aides, who was well aware of Chaplin's iconoclastic cinema. 'He's sympathetic to our cause!' 'In that case,' Gandhiji replied, 'I will meet with him.' During their brief meeting, Chaplin asked Gandhiji, 'I am all for the freedom of your country and its people. But there is one thing that I don't understand. Why do you oppose the use of machines?' Gandhiji replied frankly, 'I am not against machines, but I cannot bear it when these very machines take away a man's work from him. Today, we are your slaves because we cannot overcome our attraction for your goods. Freedom will surely be ours if we learn to free ourselves from this attraction.'

101

'Where Are Your Pants?'

In September 1931, when Gandhiji went to London to attend the Second Round Table Conference with the British government, he was the guest of the king. But he chose to leave the luxurious hotel he had been put up in, preferring to stay in the poorest part of the city. During his early morning walks on the foggy streets of London, many children followed and played with him. A few even teased him, saying, 'Hey Gandhiji, where are your pants?' Gandhiji laughed heartily at this. Some children in England gave Gandhiji toys for the poor children in India—these toys were the only gifts that he brought back with him to India.

One Is Not a Pair

In those days, it was common for the British rail company to stop a train at a station only if the whites wanted to get on or off. Once, Gandhiji had a train to catch. As he was waiting patiently on the platform, the train entered the station, but as there were no Britishers who wanted to board or disembark the train, it barely slowed down. So, Gandhiji ran after the train until he managed to get on it in the nick of time! But as he jumped on to the step of the train with one foot, the sandal from his other foot fell off. He tried to pick it up from the platform, but instead, it slipped down on to the track. He immediately turned around, took off the sandal from his other foot and threw it out! A shocked fellow passenger, who saw the whole scene, wondered why he did that. Gandhiji calmly explained, 'Well, if someone finds one of my sandals, hopefully he'll find the other one too and will have a fine new pair of sandals for himself!'

103

The King and the Mahatma

In 1931, Gandhiji wore a dhoti even when he went to meet the English king—a fact that caused much amusement in the British press. When asked later if he had worn enough clothes at the meeting, Gandhiji famously quipped, 'The king had on enough for the both of us.'

Gandhiji and Einstein

German physicist and Nobel Prize-winning scientist, Albert Einstein, once wrote to Gandhiji: 'You have shown [that] it's possible to succeed without violence, even with those who have not disregarded the method of violence. We may hope that your example will spread beyond the borders of your country and will help to establish an international authority, respected by all, which will take decisions and replace war conflicts. I hope that I will be able to meet you face to face some day.' To this, Gandhiji sent a warm reply: 'I was delighted to have your beautiful letter . . . It is a great consolation to me that the work I am doing finds favour in your sight. I do indeed wish that we could meet face to face and that too in India at my ashram.'

105

The Gift of the Gab

Gandhiji was once addressing a group of delegates in London on behalf of the people of India. He spoke eloquently for over two hours and had the audience mesmerized. After he had finished, the London reporters clustered around Gandhiji's secretary Mahadev Desai and asked him, 'How is it that Gandhi is able to speak so well for such a long time without any preparation, without any notes and without any prompting?' Desai explained, 'That's because what Gandhiji feels, what he thinks, what he says and what he does are all the same. He does not need any notes.' Then he added, 'You and I think one thing, feel another, say a third and do a fourth. So, we need notes and files to keep track.'

Cats in Prison

When Gandhiji came back from Britain, Ba informed him that the new Viceroy Lord Willingdon had arrested Nehru. Gandhiji spoke about the tyranny of the government on 28 December 1931 at Azad Maidan, for which he was arrested in the middle of one night in January 1932 in Mani Bhavan, Bombay. He was again taken to Yerwada Jail, where he was soon joined by Mahadev Desai and Vallabhbhai Patel—old friends of his. Soon, a cat came into their lives, cheering all the inmates with her playful antics. And when she had kittens, Gandhiji and his fellow inmates were provided with more than enough distraction!

107

The Mahatma and His Mindfulness

In August 1932, the British government announced the Communal Award, which granted separate electorates in India to exclude the depressed classes, now known as the scheduled caste, from the rest of the Hindu society. Gandhiji thought of the award as an attempt to divide the country according to the different communities. He decided to sit on a fast unto death in the Yerwada Jail where he was lodged at the time until the Communal Award was introduced. During the fast, Jack Winslow, an Englishman who was sympathetic towards Gandhiji's cause, went to see him. Gandhiji was lying on a cot in the open court under a tree. As Winslow was walking towards him, he unknowingly struck his head on an overhanging bough. A few days later, Winslow again went to meet Gandhiji and as he was approaching, Gandhiji raised his hand in warning and said, 'Mind the branch.' With visitors coming all day, it was amazing that Gandhiji could remember even the smallest of details about each one of them.

The Sustainable Toothbrush

One day in the Yerwada Jail, Kaka Kalelkar, a close aide of Gandhiji who was also lodged in the same jail, suggested that they should stop getting *datuns*—pieces of fresh neem or babul twigs used as toothbrushes—from outside. There were enough neem trees in the area, so Kalelkar offered to make a nice, fresh datun for Gandhiji every morning. Gandhiji gladly agreed. The next day, Kalelkar crafted a datun, pounded one end of it into a soft brush and gave it to Gandhiji. After using it, Gandhiji said, 'Now cut off the used bit of the datun and pound the end into a brush again.' Kalelkar was surprised. 'But why?' he asked. 'We can get a fresh one every day.' 'I know we can,' said Gandhiji, 'But that does not mean we should. We do not have the right. We must not fling away a datun until it becomes too dry to be used.'

109

Gita by Heart

Gandhiji had decided to memorize the complete Bhagavad Gita when he was in South Africa. There, he used to write two or three *shlokas* or couplets from the Gita on the wall and would memorize them while brushing his teeth. In Yerwada Jail, he had enough time on his hands. So, he decided to improve his pronunciation and learn the shlokas by heart. Kaka Kalelkar knew the Gita very well. So Gandhiji told him, 'Kaka, I want to learn the correct pronunciations of the shlokas in the Bhagavad Gita. I have watched you teaching the Gita to the children in the Sabarmati Ashram. Please stop me whenever I pronounce incorrectly. I would repeat it to improve the pronunciation. Don't think that I am "great" or a "mahatma". If such a thought would prevent you from correcting my pronunciation, it would be sinful on your part. Treat me like a pupil, and keep correcting me till I don't memorize it flawlessly.' Whenever Kaka Kalelkar would point out an error, Gandhiji would mark it with a pencil and read it repeatedly—and that's how Gandhiji learnt the Gita by heart.

Three Simple Words

One American journalist who was closely following Gandhiji's work once asked him, 'Can you tell me the secret of your life in three words?' 'Yes,' replied Gandhiji. 'Renounce and enjoy.' Gandhiji was quoting from the Isha Upanishad, one of the ancient Indian texts and a key scripture of the Vedanta philosophy. For Gandhiji, the entire Bhagavad Gita, with its 700 verses contained in eighteen chapters, was only a commentary on these three simple words.

111

Chicken Soup as Prescribed

Once, Dr Syed Mahmood, a well-known leader of the national struggle in Bihar, went to meet Gandhiji in the Sevagram Ashram in Maharashtra. Gandhiji found out that Dr Mahmood was quite ill. So, he asked Dr Mahmood to stay in the ashram until he was well enough to travel and bear the strain of his heavy workload. But Dr Mahmood hesitated. On Gandhiji's insistence, he explained his dilemma. He told Gandhiji that the doctor who was treating him had prescribed chicken soup in his diet as essential for recovery. Since non-vegetarian food wasn't allowed in the ashram, it would be difficult for him to stay. Gandhiji surprised him by saying, 'Would the inmates of the ashram not understand? I will see that you get well-made chicken soup every day. If the doctor prescribes something, you must have it. The ashram people may not have meat themselves, but they must learn how to feed others if and when it is absolutely essential.'

A Diet Plan for Netaji

Gandhiji was known for his experiments with food. He also wrote books on food and health like *Diet and Diet Reform*, *The Moral Basis of Vegetarianism* and *Key to Health*. Apart from his followers, Gandhiji often advised others on what to eat. In 1936, Gandhiji made a diet chart for Netaji Subhash Chandra Bose, one of his fiercest political opponents. In this chart, Gandhiji wrote:

'Leafy vegetables must be taken, better if taken as salads. Potatoes and starchy tubers should be taken sparingly. Garlic and onion in a raw state are strongly recommended in the West. I take raw garlic regularly for blood pressure. It is the best antitoxin for internal use. Dates are fine food for a healthy stomach, but raisins are more digestible. Tea and coffee I do not consider essential to health'.

117

113

Gandhiji and Hitler

Adolf Hitler, the German politician and the leader of the Nazi Party, believed the Germans were a superior race and were meant to rule the world. In one of the most horrible crimes of the world ever, he sent the German Jews, whom he considered an inferior race, to concentration camps where six million Jews were killed. In July 1939, Gandhiji wrote a letter to Hitler, asking him to 'prevent a war which may reduce humanity to a savage state'.

The Half-Naked Fakir

The British statesman, Winston Churchill, who as the prime minister (1940–45 and 1951–55) led the British people to victory during World War II, once contemptuously called Gandhiji a half-naked fakir, referring to Gandhiji's habit of dressing only in a dhoti. Unfazed by this, Gandhiji used the phrase in a letter to Churchill in 1944.

Dear Prime Minister,

You are reported to have the desire to crush the "half-naked fakir", as you are said to have described me. I have long been trying to be a fakir and then naked—a more difficult task. I, therefore, regard the expression as a compliment, though unintended. I approach you, then, as such and ask you to trust and use me for the sake of your people and through them, those of the world.

Your sincere friend,
M.K. Gandhi

115

A Salt-Free Diet

In 1913, Ba was ill. Gandhiji entreated her to give up salt and pulses as a part of her treatment. But she did not agree even when Gandhiji pleaded with her. At last, she challenged him saying that even he could not give up those articles if he was advised to do so. Gandhiji was pained. He told her, 'You're mistaken. If I was ailing and the doctor advised me to give up those articles, I should unhesitatingly do so. Now, without any medical advice, I am giving up salt and pulses whether you do so or not.' Kasturba was shocked and exclaimed, 'Knowing you, I shouldn't have provoked you! I promise to abstain from these things. But for heaven's sake, take back your vow. It is too hard on me.' Gandhiji said, 'It is very good for you to forgo these articles. I have not the slightest doubt that you will be all the better without them. As for me, I cannot retract the vow seriously taken. And it is sure to benefit me; for any restraint, whatever prompts it, is wholesome for me. It will be a test for me and a moral support to you in carrying out your resolve.'

120

What Gandhiji Ate

Gandhiji preferred eating simple vegetarian meals and fruits. His meals were cooked without salt, sugar, oil, chillies or other spices. His day began with a glass of lukewarm water and honey. His lunch included roti with vegetables and goat milk. With his meals, he liked chutney made from neem leaves and garlic. Among fruits, he preferred oranges, apples, grapes and mangoes. The butter he had was quite unique—he added fried groundnut to bananas and called it butter! His dessert would usually be a small chunk of palm jaggery.

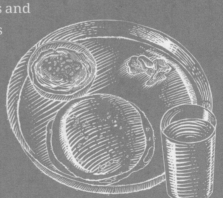

117

Gandhiji, the Label Checker

Gandhiji was very particular about what he ate and avoided foods made from ingredients he couldn't pronounce. In the 1930s, when Indian companies began importing low-fat substitutes to ghee (clarified butter), many thought that he'd be among the first to accept them. But Gandhiji was quick to prove them wrong. Since these substitutes were made in a factory, Gandhiji rejected them, stating they were unhealthy.

The Mahatma's Love for Mangoes

Throughout his life, Gandhiji tried to not eat too much of anything. He believed that excessive consumption of food could distract him from his spiritual goals. One of the things that he kept strictly out of his diet was sugar. But there was one sweet fruit that he had a special weakness for—mangoes. Once, he received a crate of fresh mangoes as medicine for a group of patients he was helping and he entirely gave in. Gandhiji, known for his restraint against cravings, ate many mangoes before sending the boxes off to the patients. He repented his indulgence later in a letter. 'Mango is a cursed fruit,' Gandhiji wrote in 1941. 'It attracts attention as no other fruit does. We must get used to not treating it with so much affection . . . but they [the patients] will all get some as we still have some left in the three boxes.'

A Child at Heart

You might have seen a photograph of Gandhiji rubbing noses with a baby and another one where a little boy is holding his walking stick and leading him. Gandhiji was very fond of children—they were his friends and playmates. At Sabarmati Ashram, he had a group of children he used to play with—he called them his *vanar sena* or army of monkeys. He taught them how to spin cotton on a charkha and took them for swimming in the river. Horace Alexander, a British teacher, writer and ornithologist, was once visiting the Sabarmati Ashram. He noticed that Gandhiji was playing with children even when he was working. While each member of the ashram gave his or her report to Gandhiji on the quantity of cotton spun, the children ran playfully around Gandhiji while he thrust out his hand as if to catch them.

The Three Famous Monkeys

Have you heard of how Gandhiji acquired the three famous monkeys?

One day, a group of visitors had arrived from China, visiting Gandhiji.

'Gandhiji, we have brought you a small gift,' they said. 'It is very popular in our country.'

Gandhiji was delighted to see what the gift was—a set of the three monkeys that were to become so iconic all over the world. Gandhiji named them Bapu, Ketan and Bandar.

121

Gandhiji's Watch

Gandhiji possessed a pocket watch—sometimes he kept it on his table, sometimes he tucked it inside the folds of his dhoti and at other times, he gently held it up to his visitors when they showed no signs of getting up and leaving, even after the time he'd given them was over. One day, a child named Pratap and his mother, who lived in the Sabarmati Ashram, were standing in front of Gandhiji. The child's eyes shone at the sight of the dangling golden chain and the watch. He wanted to have them and began tugging at his mother's saree again and again. Sizing the situation, Gandhiji walked up to the child and put the watch against his ears. As the child listened intently to the tick-tock sound of the watch, he said to the child, 'Hear, how well it ticks!' Then he took the watch away from the child's ear and said, 'You have your toys. I have mine. This is my toy. So, you should not ask for it.'

Sweet Tooth

One morning, a woman came to Gandhiji. Her son was also with her. 'My son eats too many sweets every day. I try to stop him, but he doesn't listen to me at all. He respects you a lot. Will you please tell him to stop eating sweets?' she said. 'Come after three months,' Gandhiji said. The woman could not understand why Gandhiji could not tell her son to stop eating sweets at that very moment. After three months, she and her son came to Gandhiji again. This time, Gandhiji explained to the boy that eating too many sweets is bad for his health. 'Why didn't you tell him the same thing three months back?' the woman asked Gandhiji. 'How could I,' he said, 'when three months back, I myself was eating a lot of sweets? I wanted to first stop it myself and then tell your son.'

123

The Virtue of Orderliness

On one occasion, Gandhiji wanted to write something down and was looking for the pencil that he had kept on the right side of his desk. He could not find it and was a little annoyed. He called his secretary who pointed out that the pencil was on the left side of the desk. When Gandhiji was alone, one of his assistants asked him if a small pencil was the reason for his annoyance. Wasn't it too trifling a matter? Gandhiji replied calmly, 'There must be orderliness in one's life. If the sun, the moon and the earth do not observe their laws, the entire universe would collapse. Every minute of mine is scheduled for certain duties. If I do not find my things in their proper place, much of my time would be wasted, much inconvenience would be caused and my work would greatly suffer. My near ones should bear these things in mind.'

Gandhiji and His Goat

Gandhiji had a pet goat named Nirmala. He once had a very important meeting in the Sabarmati Ashram with three renowned British politicians. As the meeting gathered steam, Gandhiji suddenly got up and left the room. He went to the backyard to apply a soft mud pack over Nirmala's sprained leg. The Englishmen followed Gandhiji and they fumed in anger after what they saw. 'It surprises me no end that Gandhi had to break the decorum of a meeting for such a trifle!' one of them said in a disgusted voice. Maulana Azad, who was standing nearby, remarked, 'It is, in fact, these trifles that have made Gandhiji a mahatma.'

A Minute Less

Once, Gandhiji's eldest grandson, Kantilal, was sitting next to him. Gandhiji was writing something, when suddenly he asked Kantilal what the time was. Kantilal looked at the wristwatch he was wearing and told him that it was five o'clock. From the corner of his eyes, Gandhiji also looked at Kantilal's watch and noticed that there was still a minute to five. He stopped writing and exclaimed, 'Is it five?' Kantilal was embarrassed. He said, 'No, Bapu. It is one minute to five.' 'Well, Kanti,' Gandhiji said, 'what is the use of keeping a wristwatch? You have no value of time. Do you know how many days or months minutes like these would make? What a colossal waste of time it would mean for our poor country? You don't respect truth as you know it. Would it have cost you more energy to say, "It is one minute to five" than to say, "It is five o'clock?"'

The Last Bell

Gandhiji was extremely punctual. His Ingersoll pocket watch never left his side. In Sabarmati Ashram, too, punctuality was strictly enforced. The rules laid it out that when the last bell for prayer rang, the gates to the prayer ground would be closed. No one who came late would be admitted. One day, Gandhiji was busy with some visitors and started for the prayer a little late. The last bell rang as he was crossing the gate. One of his feet was inside and the other one out. The gatekeeper waited for an extra second to let Gandhiji in. But Gandhiji was full of remorse. At the end of the prayer, he said, 'I have been a defaulter today. Though most of my body was inside, yet, one foot remained outside. So, the gatekeeper ought not to have shown me favour. I also should have stayed out. However, I was moved by the thought that so many of you would be waiting for me. But such consideration should not be shown to anyone except a sick person or his attendant nor should one accept such preferential treatment.'

127

Naptime for Bapu

Gandhiji kept a minute-by-minute record of his day. While he himself kept a mental account, his secretaries maintained a written account. Since he was always hard-pressed for time, whether he was in his ashram or on his whirlwind tours, he developed the habit of taking naps wherever he could, so as to prevent the strain to take a toll on his health. Once, Gandhiji was touring Tamil Nadu to campaign against untouchability and had to cover many miles to go from one meeting to another. He was travelling by car and had enough time to catch up on his sleep. As he sat into the car, he asked his associate, Dr Rajan, who was in-charge of the tour, 'Well, Rajan, what is the next item on my schedule—a ten- or fifteen-minute nap?' Dr Rajan replied, 'Well, Bapu, the next item is a good thirty-minute nap!' 'What a luxury!' Gandhiji exclaimed and, within minutes, he was fast asleep. He woke up, punctual to the minute, as the car came to a stop at the venue of the next gathering, as awake and alert as ever.

Every Minute Counts

This happened when Gandhiji was travelling in the toy train in Darjeeling. As the train was moving up the hill, suddenly, the engine got detached from the coaches. So, the engine went ahead while the coaches slid backwards. There was a huge panic and the people inside the train were terrified. While all this was going on, Gandhiji was calmly dictating letters to his secretary. After a while, the secretary said, 'Bapu, do you know what's happening? We are hanging between life and death! We don't even know whether we will be alive the next moment or not!' Do you know what Mahatma Gandhi said in reply? He said, 'If we die, we die. But if we are saved, we'd have wasted so much time! So, please take the dictation.' With trembling hands, Gandhiji's secretary took the dictation. And, well, they did get saved after all!

129

Water Is Precious

Once, Gandhiji's grand-nephew Kanubhai and grandson Kantilal were cleaning utensils at a well. Gandhiji happened to pass that way and saw them pouring a copious amount of water to clean a small vessel. He went to them and said, 'Look here, how much water you two are wasting!' 'Well, Bapu,' they argued, 'it is our energy that is spent in drawing more water.' Gandhiji gently said, 'Quite right, but why do you forget that here we live for the service of the others? Can you waste your energy like this? No, you must preserve it for the service of our country.' Then, Gandhiji sat down and showed them how to clean utensils with the minimum quantity of water. 'See, take a small quantity of wet earth and rub it all over the vessel, then put plenty of dry earth in the vessel and clean the vessel dry. After this, you don't require a large quantity of water to wash it. Now, will you clean the utensils like this?' he asked them both. They promised to wash the utensils as instructed by Gandhiji, but he did not budge from where he was until he'd seen the children perform their duty well.

The Ingenious Envelopes

One day, Krishnadas, who was working as Gandhiji's secretary during the days of the Non-Cooperation Movement, found him in a happy mood. As soon as he entered Bapu's room, he told him, 'Krishnadas, so many telegrams come to me daily, and yet not knowing what to do with the forms, I used to tear them. But I was not happy that I had to tear them and I was thinking of what use they could be put to. At last, I have hit upon a plan.' Bapu took up a form and demonstrated to Krishnadas how to make an envelope out of it. He then instructed his secretary to make envelopes from the telegraph forms he received every day. Gandhiji called these envelopes his 'patent envelopes' and would not use any other envelope as long as these were available.

131

The Fourth Class

During British rule in India, the trains were divided into three classes. The luxurious first-class compartments were for the British. The comfortable second-class compartments were used by the rich Indians, and the dirty, wooden benches that formed the third-class compartments were for the vast majority of the economically weaker Indians. Gandhiji always preferred to travel third class. Someone once asked him, 'Bapu, why do you always travel in third class?' Gandhiji quipped immediately, 'Because there's no fourth class!'

Service before Self

Once, Gandhiji and his associates had to go to Bengal. Two third-class compartments were booked for them. When Gandhiji came to the station, he found that his party could be accommodated in a single compartment and the other compartment wasn't required at all. So, he called his grand-nephew, who was looking after the arrangements of the journey and asked him to vacate one of the compartments.

His grand-nephew told Gandhiji that both the compartments were reserved for the party and the reservation charges had already been paid. 'That does not matter,' replied Gandhiji. 'We are going to Bengal for the service of the poor and the starving millions. It does not behove us to enjoy comforts on the train . . . Travelling third class with so many reservations would be a criminal joke.' The whole party was then moved to one compartment and the other compartment was vacated for other passengers.

137

133

Who Saw Gandhiji?

Gandhiji was once visiting the Harijan Ashram in Delhi. Many workshops on vocational skills to train young boys were held in this ashram. When Gandhiji entered one workshop during his round of inspection, all the boys stopped working and stared at Gandhiji. But there was this one boy who was so engrossed in making rotis that he did not see Gandhiji standing right in front of him. As Gandhiji came out of the workshop, one of the boys remarked, 'Arrey, the boy who was making rotis did not see Bapu at all.' Bapu responded at once, 'If there was anyone in the workshop who really saw me, it was the boy who was making rotis.'

The Strength of Self-Reliance

Gandhiji was once in Calcutta (now Kolkata). He was staying in a newly built building of an educational society and a young associate had been assigned the duty of looking after Gandhiji. One morning, when Gandhiji stepped out with a mug, a bar of soap and a towel for his bath, the young man rushed to him and asked if he could carry his stuff to the bathroom. Gandhiji gently told him that what he was carrying was not too heavy. 'Can I be allowed to wash your clothes then?' asked the associate. Gandhiji declined politely, saying, 'I do it myself every day.'

135

The Mahatma and the Maharajahs

Gandhiji was once giving a lecture to a select gathering of maharajahs, urging them to give up their treasures and live a life of simplicity. Slowly, his distinguished audience melted away until only Gandhiji and the chairman were left. A little later, Gandhiji remarked that there was nobody in this room 'except God, the chairman and myself.' A few minutes later, the chairman also slid away. 'Poor fellow,' Gandhi chuckled, 'he must have been very uncomfortable in that strange company!'

Cricket and Politics

Once, the Nawab of Pataudi went to pay a visit to Gandhiji. Wanting a change from the usual discussion topics, Gandhiji suddenly told him that he had made up his mind to challenge him to a game of single wicket cricket. He asked the nawab if he would accept the challenge. The nawab replied that he would, but on one condition—when the match would be over, he would be allowed to challenge Gandhiji in politics. The nawab proceeded to tell Gandhiji, wearing a serious expression, that just as he was certain that Gandhiji would beat him at cricket, he was equally certain that he would beat Gandhiji in politics. Gandhiji laughed like a child, patted the nawab affectionately on his back and said, 'Nawab Sahib, you have bowled me out already.'

137

Of Dangerous Dacoits

There was a time when the Singoli area of Gwalior was a thick jungle, ruled by gangs of dangerous dacoits. It was impossible to pass through the jungle without armed guards. One day, a goldsmith went to one of Gandhiji's associates, Shri Ram Narain Chaudhari and thanked him profusely. Chaudhari could not recall doing anything for the goldsmith and he wanted to know why the goldsmith was thanking him. The goldsmith then told him about the time when he was passing through the Singoli jungle and was caught by the dacoits. He had greeted them with a slogan of 'Vande Mataram' and told them that he was Gandhiji's follower. On hearing this, the dacoits left him alone and withdrew into the jungle. On another occasion, Chaudhari himself was passing through the jungle with some peasants when a gang of dacoits advanced towards them. The peasants shouted, 'Mahatma Gandhi ki jai!' after which the gang retreated into the jungle.

Gandhiji and the Thief

Once, Gandhiji's watch got stolen from his railway compartment when he was travelling to Delhi. Gandhiji was upset. But almost six months later, a man came to see Gandhiji in Birla House where he was staying. At first, he refused to give his name or tell Gandhiji's secretary the reason for his insistence on meeting him. Finally, he admitted that he'd stolen Gandhiji's watch and that he had come to return it and ask for forgiveness. 'Forgive you?' exclaimed the secretary. 'He will embrace you!' He took the man to Gandhiji. And sure enough, Gandhiji hugged this man and, giggling like a child who'd found his lost toy, called all his followers to meet this great man who'd returned his watch.

Bapu and Sarojini Naidu

Once, a function was organized in the Sevagram Ashram to collect donations for the Kasturba Gandhi National Memorial Trust. A woman came with a collection of Rs 1,00,000 kept in her purse. She stretched out her hand holding the purse towards Gandhiji. When Gandhiji was about to take the purse from her, she withdrew her hand and said, 'Bapu, suppose I run away with the purse, what will you do?' Everyone around them was taken aback by the woman's words. But Gandhiji was unperturbed. He smiled and said, 'I know you are capable of doing what you've said. But I have nothing to worry about, for I know pretty well that you will utilize the money for a noble, charitable purpose only.' This woman, who was in the habit of playing practical jokes on a person like Gandhiji, was none other than Sarojini Naidu, the famous poet and a great patriot.

A Royal Wedding Gift

It was the day of the royal wedding. Princess Elizabeth, the eldest daughter of King George VI, and Prince Philip, the Duke of Edinburgh, would get married at Westminster Abbey on 20 November 1947. The princess received the most precious wedding gifts from around the world. Among them was one gift that Lord Mountbatten, the last viceroy of India, gave to the bride. It was a gift from Mahatma Gandhi—a simple khadi shawl. The cloth was woven from yarn specially spun by Gandhiji and bore the words 'Jai Hind'. In 2007, when Queen Elizabeth II celebrated the sixtieth anniversary of her marriage to Prince Philip, the khadi shawl was one of the gifts showcased in the London exhibition of her wedding dresses and the most treasured wedding presents.

141

Message of Communal Harmony

Once, Gandhiji was leading a peace march in the riot-hit area of Noakhali in Bengal. When he was walking in the Babu Bazaar area, a fanatic stifled his throat and pushed him on the ground. Gandhiji started reciting 'Surah Al-Fatihah', which he'd memorized from the Koran. The offender was astonished to hear such a fine recital of the Koran from a Hindu's mouth and apologized profusely for his actions. The man, Allahdad Khan Mondol, became one of the most trusted disciples of Gandhiji. Gandhiji also advised the Hindus and the Muslims to be tight-lipped about this incident, lest the harmony of the place be disturbed.

146

The Mahatma's Musical Interests

142

Gandhiji had many interests. He liked to listen to classical music and was an admirer of the legendary singer M.S. Subbulakshmi. In 1947, just a few months after Independence, Gandhiji wanted her to record his favourite bhajan 'Hari Tum Haro' and send it to Delhi for him to listen. But she said that she was not familiar with this song and perhaps some other singer could render it. But Gandhiji refused and said that he would rather have Subbulakshmi stammer while singing the bhajan than have anyone else sing it. So, she recorded the bhajan overnight on a cassette, which was sent to Delhi by an aeroplane for Gandhiji. A few months after that, while listening to All India Radio, the singer heard the news of Gandhiji's assassination, after which she heard her own voice and the bhajan 'Hari Tum Haro'. Deeply shaken by this tragic news, she fainted.

147

143

Gandhiji's Last Birthday: 2 October 1947

It was Gandhiji's first birthday after India gained independence. Gandhiji spent the day fasting, praying, reading and spinning yarn. He transformed that birthday into a celebration of the spinning wheel—the symbol of peace and non-violence. Pandit Nehru, Sardar Patel, his host Ghanshyamdas Birla and many political leaders came to wish him. One of the visitors jokingly said, 'Bapuji, on our birthdays, we touch your feet; on your birthday too, we have to touch your feet. How is that fair?' Gandhiji smiled and said, 'The ways of mahatmas are always different. That is not my fault. You people have wrongly declared me a mahatma, now bear the consequences!'

Gandhiji's Last Day

Gandhiji was staying in Birla House in Delhi. Friday, 30 January 1948, was like any other day, with no one knowing what was to happen in the evening. Conditions in Delhi were troubled those days. There had been a bomb explosion at the prayer meeting in Birla House on 20 January. The security at Birla House, therefore, had been increased, but Gandhiji refused the suggestion that all visitors be searched. 'Those who preferred security to freedom had no right to live,' he said. He had called Sardar Patel for a meeting at 4 p.m.; prayers were scheduled to start at 5 p.m. The discussion continued beyond 5 p.m. and Gandhiji was late by fifteen minutes for the prayer meeting. There were about 250 people awaiting his arrival. He was upset about being late. He walked briskly towards the prayer platform and . . .

145

The Fatal Shots

Gandhiji climbed the steps leading to the prayer platform. People made way for him to go to the wooden dais. The assassin, Nathuram Godse, had been waiting in this crowd, hiding a revolver in his clothes. Gandhiji had walked hardly five or six paces towards the dais when Godse stepped out of the crowd flanking Gandhiji's path and fired some shots in quick succession from close range, resulting in the Mahatma's instantaneous death. He fell down, bleeding profusely. The end of the Mahatma, the end of hope . . .

Premonition?

In his last few days, Gandhiji had been expressing the wish that God take him away since he did not want to be a silent witness to the horrible things that were going on in the country. Margaret Bourke White, a renowned photographer for LIFE magazine, asked Gandhiji during her conversation with him on 30 January 1948 before the tragedy occurred, 'You have always stated that you would like to live up to the age of 125. What gives you that hope?' Gandhiji surprised her by answering that he no longer wished for that. When questioned why, he replied, 'Because of the terrible happenings in the world. I do not want to live in darkness.'

147

Immediate Aftermath

The news of Gandhiji's death spread like wildfire. A huge crowd gathered outside Birla House within minutes. The gates had to be closed to prevent people from entering the premises. Gandhiji's body was carried to his room. There he lay on the mat, looking as if he was asleep. Outside, there was a scramble from the public to possess something that belonged to Gandhiji as a keepsake. People started scooping out handfuls of earth from the spot where Gandhiji fell, leaving a big pit there within hours. Arrangements were then made to have the area cordoned off and a guard was posted there.

Gandhiji in Uganda

Gandhiji had spent a large part of his life in Africa. As per his wish, after his death in 1948, his ashes were divided to be scattered in several of the world's great rivers. Some of his ashes were scattered at the source of the River Nile at Jinja, Uganda. There is a bronze statue at the spot—donated by the Indian government—that commemorates the act. It is placed right near the gurgling river among lush vegetation and many trees. The plaque below reads: 'Universal apostle of peace and non-violence whose ashes were immersed in the River Nile in 1948'.

An Inspiration to Many

Martin Luther King Jr, the great leader of the civil rights movement to bring equality to African-American people in the US, used similar methods of civil disobedience as Gandhiji. He regarded the Mahatma's teachings as his guiding light. He furthered it by adding, 'From my background, I gained my regulating Christian ideals. From Gandhi, I learned my operational technique.'

Barack Obama, who made history by becoming the first African-American President of the US in 2009, has often talked about the influence Gandhiji had on his life. He often quotes Gandhiji as his inspiration to spread the message that we be the change we seek in the world. He was also quoted as saying, 'I might not be standing before you today, as President of the United States, had it not been for Gandhi and the message he shared.'

In Honour of . . .

As a way of honouring the legacy left behind by Gandhiji, in 2007, the United Nations declared his birthday to be established as the International Day of Non-Violence. In honour of the 150th birth anniversary of Gandhiji in 2019, Magyar Posta issued a commemorative miniature sheet designed by the graphic artist Eszter Domé on 21 February. As many as 40,000 copies of the miniature sheet were printed. The miniature sheet contains four identical stamps on which Gandhiji is doing namaskar.

With the 58th edition of the international art exhibition (11 May to 24 November 2019), titled May You Live in Interesting Times, India returns to the Venice Biennale after an eight-year gap with a pavilion themed on 150 years of Gandhi. It showcases Gandhi-themed works by artists, including Atul Dodiya, G.R. Iranna, Jitish Kallat, Shakuntala Kulkarni, Ashim Purkayastha, Nandalal Bose and Rummana Hussain.

TRIVIA AND MORE

Gandhiji's Family Tree

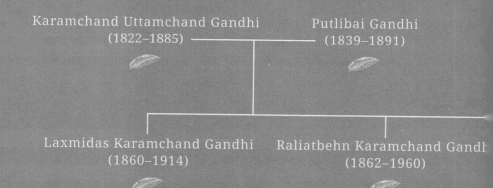

Karamchand Uttamchand Gandhi
(1822–1885)

Putlibai Gandhi
(1839–1891)

Laxmidas Karamchand Gandhi
(1860–1914)

Raliatbehn Karamchand Gandhi
(1862–1960)

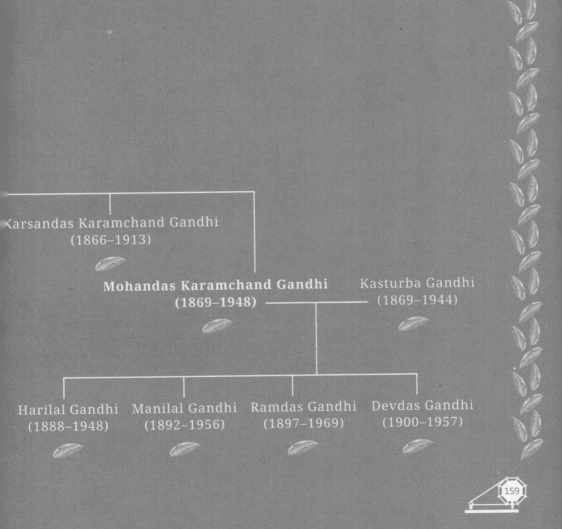

Karsandas Karamchand Gandhi
(1866–1913)

Mohandas Karamchand Gandhi
(1869–1948) ——————— Kasturba Gandhi
(1869–1944)

Harilal Gandhi   Manilal Gandhi   Ramdas Gandhi   Devdas Gandhi
(1888–1948)   (1892–1956)   (1897–1969)   (1900–1957)

Timeline

1869 Mohandas Karamchand Gandhi is born in Porbandar, Gujarat.

1883 Gandhiji is married to Kasturba Makhanji.

1888 Gandhiji leaves for England to study law.

1893 Gandhiji sails to South Africa for work. He experiences racial discrimination and decides to protest against it.

1894 Gandhiji forms the Natal Indian Congress to fight discrimination against Indians in South Africa.

1903 Gandhiji starts a newspaper for Indians in South Africa called the *Indian Opinion*.

1904 Gandhiji opens Phoenix Farm in Durban.

1907 The first Satyagraha takes place at Transvaal, South Africa.

1910 Gandhiji establishes Tolstoy Farm near Johannesburg.

1914 Gandhiji returns to India and travels the length and breadth of the country.

1917 Gandhiji establishes the Sabarmati Ashram in Ahmedabad. He also starts the Champaran Satyagraha campaign for the rights of indigo farmers in Bihar.

1920 Gandhiji launches the Non-Cooperation movement.

1930 Gandhiji leads the Dandi March and starts the Civil Disobedience Movement.

1933 Gandhiji establishes the Sevagram Ashram in Wardha, Maharashtra.

1942 Gandhiji launches the Quit India movement in Bombay, is arrested and imprisoned with Kasturba Gandhi.

1944 Kasturba Gandhi dies in prison.

1947 India gains independence. Gandhiji is in Calcutta, working towards restoring communal harmony post the Partition of India.

1948 Gandhiji is assassinated by Nathuram Godse.

Museums and Memorials of the Mahatma

All across India, there are many museums and memorials that have an amazing archive of Gandhiji's writings, photographs and objects belonging to him like his clothes, walking stick, spectacles, etc. If you want to know more about Gandhiji, you can visit the following museums and memorials.

- Gandhi Smriti and Darshan Samiti, New Delhi
- National Gandhi Museum, Rajghat, New Delhi
- Sabarmati Ashram and museum, Ahmedabad
- Dandi Kutir, Gandhinagar
- Kirti Mandir and museum, Porbandar
- Gandhi Smarak Sangrahalaya, Barrackpore, West Bengal
- Gandhi Memorial Museum, Madurai
- Gandhi Sangrahalaya, Patna
- Gandhi National Memorial Society, Pune
- Mani Bhavan Gandhi Sangrahalaya, Mumbai

Selected Bibliography

- Chaudhury, Ramnarayan. *Bapu as I Saw Him*. Ahmedabad: Navjivan Trust, 1959.
- Fischer, Louis. *The Life of Mahatma Gandhi*. New York, Evanston, London: Harper & Row, 1950.
- Gandhi, M.K. *Introduction to An Autobiography or The Story of My Experiments with Truth* (Critical Edition) by Tridip Suhrud. Gurgaon: Penguin Random House India, 2018.
- Horace, Alexander. *Gandhi through Western Eyes*. Philadelphia: New Society Publishers, 1984.
- Kapoor, Pramod. *Gandhi: An Illustrated Biography*. New Delhi: Roli Books, 2017.
- Polak, Millie Graham. *Mr Gandhi: The Man*. Bombay: Vora and Company, 1949.
- Quinn, Jason. *Gandhi: My Life is My Message*. New Delhi: Campfire, 2014.
- Tendulkar, D.G. *Mahatma: Life of Mohandas Karamchand Gandhi*. New Delhi: Publications Division, Ministry of Information and Broadcasting, Government of India, 1961.